Classroom Interviews

Classroom Interviews

A World of Learning

Paula Rogovin

HEINEMANN
Portsmouth, NH

Heinemann
A division of Reed Elsevier Inc.
361 Hanover Street
Portsmouth, NH 03801-3912
Offices and agents throughout the world.

We would like to thank those who have given their permission to include material in this book.

"A Worker Reads History" by Bertolt Brecht from *Selected Poems, Bertolt Brecht*. Copyright © H. R. Hays, Editor. Reprinted by permission of Ann Elmo Agency, Inc.

Figure on page 15 adapted from *Caribbean Connections*. Copyright © 1991. Used by permission of Ecumenical Program on Central America (EPICA), 1470 Irving Street, NW, Washington, D.C. 20010.

"The Palet Man" from *A Coconut Kind of Day* by Lynn Joseph. Copyright © 1990. Reprinted by permission of Lothrop, Lee, and Shepard Books, A Division of William Morrow & Company, Inc.

"Dreams" from *Collected Poems* by Langston Hughes. Copyright © 1994 by the Estate of Langston Hughes. Reprinted by permission of Alfred A Knopf Inc and Harold Ober Associates Incorporated.

Library of Congress Cataloging-in-Publication Data
Rogovin, Paula.
    Classroom interviews: a world of learning / by Paula Rogovin
        p.   cm.
    Includes bibliographical references.
    ISBN 0-325-00047-6
    1. Education, Primary—Activity programs—United States.
    2. Interviewing—Study and teaching (Primary)—United States.
    3. Community—Study and teaching (Primary)—United States.
    4. Curriculum planning—United States.   5. Language experience
approach in education—United States.   I. Title.
    LB1537.R652   1998
    372.19—dc21   98-10079
                                                                CIP

On the cover: Moises, Almedina, and Katherine with Dr. Winifred Latimer Norman, granddaughter of the inventor Lewis Latimer, after an interview.

Editor: Lois Bridges
Production: Renée Le Verrier
Cover design: Barbara Werden
Manufacturing: Louise Richardson

Printed in the United States of America on acid-free paper.

02 01 00 99 98 DA 1 2 3 4 5

I dedicate this book to my mother and father, Anne and Milton Rogovin,
my three sons, David, Steven, and Eric,
my sister, Ellen, her daughters, Malaika and Aliya, and her granddaughter, Hoshea,
and my brother, Mark.
I love you.

Contents

Foreword

Invite Paula Rogovin to join the teaching staff of your school and watch the walls come down between school and community.

Some days you will have to work hard to find Paula and her team of first graders. They might be out-of-doors, taking notes at a local construction site, visiting a parent's shoemaker shop, delivering cans of food to the local soup kitchen, or planting gardenias in the flower boxes they've placed in the windows of our school's cafeteria. On other days you'll find them at home, in marvelously cluttered and cozy room 407.

The minute you walk in, the children will welcome you, eager to share what they are learning. Everyone is a teacher in Paula's classroom. Her students are always ready to tell you about the snakes, rabbit, frogs, snails, and turtles that line the counters in their classroom. They are eager to share the constructions in their block corner. They like to explain their replicas of the Underground Railroad, sweatshops filled with child laborers, the Chunnel that connects England to France and the baseball stadium in which Jackie Robinson made civil rights history. They will show you a striking photograph from *National Geographic*, demonstrate a collection of toys they've made from recycled materials, or explain the artifacts they've collected for their study of students who come from the Caribbean islands.

They'll offer you snacks—often foods made by family members—and treat you to their very own hootenanny as Paula strums her guitar. They'll eagerly show you the larger-than-life murals they are painting, depicting what it might have been like to be a farmer growing peanuts during the time of George Washington Carver, or a student in our school at the turn of the century, or an artist whose works hang in the nearby Metropolitan Museum of Art. The children might invite you to step into the hallway to hear them recite their favorite poems by Langston Hughes, Marilyn Singer, Eloise Greenfield, or Monica Gunning.

More likely than not when you enter room 407, Paula and her students will be gathered on the carpeted meeting area, all eyes on the guest of honor sitting in the corner rocking chair. There is nothing as intriguing, almost mesmerizing, as watching Paula help her students interview a class visitor. You won't be able to resist peeking over shoulders, trying to see what those very young children are writing in their stenographers' pads.

This book, detailing how Paula teaches, is long overdue, for several reasons. First, she teaches us how to tap resources. I have watched Paula and her children interview famous guests. Jackie Robinson's widow, Rachel Robinson, has sat in the visitor's chair, as have one of the Harlem Globe Trotters, a former member of the Alvin Ailey dance troupe, and a newspaper reporter about to leave for South Africa to cover the election of Nelson Mandela. Paula knows how to tap resources from far and wide, and perhaps more important, she knows how to tap resources from our own school community. She knows how to get people's stories. She helps us to see the heroes among us. She has revealed our school aide to be a local historian and our security guard to be a civil rights hero, and countless parents are now revered for the work they do in our city.

Second, Paula has discovered a way to turn those children's interview journals into the centerpiece for learning reading, writing, and social studies in her primary classroom. Flip through any child's journal and you are reading a literacy timeline. Children who remembered an interview by drawing stick figures in September are taking copious notes in June. And it's no surprise. After all, Paula has given them real reasons to write. They are fascinated with their visitors' life stories and are eager to teach others what they have learned. Then, too, they interview more than forty people a year. How can you not grow when you have such ample opportunity for repeat performances? It is too rare in the hustle and bustle of most schools to carve out time to get better and better at just one thing. Paula reminds us to trust in the power of predictable routines and teaching techniques that work. We need not dazzle children by constantly inventing new ways of doing things. Paula's children are engaged in their learning because the content is so rich and the classroom way of life is so comfortable.

Third, in this book, Paula demonstrates how to turn a visitor's sophisticated concepts and conversations into accessible information for young children. She knows how and when to graciously interrupt her visitors and slow down the flow of their information. In an instant, she has children dramatizing scenes in factories, offices, mines, farms, shops, hospitals, hotels, anywhere the telling moments of a guest's life have taken place. She knows how and when to post key words, give children time to jot notes, and ask them to turn and whisper their concerns to one another. Then, too, this book explains Paula's techniques for turning interview notes into class books, with a page written by every child. It demonstrates how those books become material for small-group reading sessions. The children can read the words because the words are their own. The children can understand the concepts because they have recorded the visitor's life through dramatization, improvisation, sketching, and storytelling.

And finally, this book will help educators realize that interviewing family and community members effects social change. Paula's classroom is not just content-rich, it is community-rich. When children bring home individual copies of those beautifully bound books about one another's parents, grandparents, neighbors, and friends, everyone marvels at one another's lives. Everyone feels grateful to be in one another's company. Everyone turns out for the evening family celebrations, eager to match the faces with the stories they have been reading, quick to hug one another, to exchange phone numbers, and to plan even more social gatherings. Knowing one another's stories changes relationships in a school community. It's no wonder family members feel privileged to have a child in Paula Rogovin's class. Their children are learning, and they are learning alongside them.

Readers, too, will feel privileged to read her words and get to know this talented colleague, family educator, and humanitarian.

Shelley Harwayne

Principal
Manhattan New School
New York City

Preface

It was always my dream to be a teacher. School would be a joyous place where children learned to read and write and become math thinkers. As they did that, they would learn about the world.

Simply to teach children to read, write, and count is not enough for me. That goal is not enough to make me excited—to make me spend hundreds of hours researching, planning, gathering materials, talking to colleagues and families in the service of my teaching. For me, there is a higher goal.

Perhaps the classroom can be a model for the world we would like to create. Then the children, our future, can go on to help create that world. Inquiry-based multicultural education is a grounding for them to do so.

At the supper table of my youth, rousing discussions abounded: politics, poetry, art, photography, science, the disabled, diverse cultures and economic classes, the war in Vietnam and marches against it—all were talked about with passion backed by concrete experiences. The basics at our table—nourishment, bonding, sharing, asking questions, seeking answers, broadening our horizons, examining multiple perspectives, planning social action—these are the concerns of inquiry-based multicultural education.

Inquiry-based multicultural education isn't popular in many school districts. There are no ready-made curriculum guides. Few teachers had an inquiry-based multicultural education themselves. How many were encouraged to ask questions or hear differing perspectives in elementary school? Certainly the schools I attended in Buffalo, New York, provided a very narrow view of history and culture. In college the focus of our core curriculum was Western Civilization. How then should teachers get the education they need to provide inquiry-based multicultural education to their students? We must think of ourselves as learners: read, observe, and learn from others.

Some say that inquiry-based multicultural education is too political. But all teaching is political because it involves choices. Choosing to encourage children to ask questions is a political choice. Choosing not to teach something in social studies is a political choice. For example, through all my years in school, we sang songs and heard stories from the cultures of the United States and Europe but never once from Africa, South America, or Asia. Africa was mentioned only as a place that European explorers had taken over. Our textbooks treasured Christopher Columbus as a hero but told nothing of what the Arawak or the Taino thought when Columbus kissed their land and said it now belonged to Spain. Those were political decisions of the local board of education at that time.

In first and second grades I studied about "community helpers": policemen, firemen, mailmen, and garbage men. How did we come to have police officers, firefighters, letter carriers, and sanitation workers? How did women get these jobs? During each period in history, those who create the standard curriculum, who write or choose textbooks, who train new teachers, determine what is important or correct to teach.

When I started teaching in 1970, the syllabus provided by the New York City Board of Education was similar to what I had learned as a child. It instructed us to teach about the nuclear family—mother, father, and children. Each had jobs to do as part of the family. Yet, when I looked around my classroom and saw children in families torn apart by economic instability, divorce, death, and immigration, I knew something was wrong with the standard syllabus. In 1970 teaching that families come in different shapes and sizes was a risky political choice. But I acknowledged in the classroom the reality of my children's lives and the lives of other children around the world.

Inquiring, examining, and challenging the status quo are essential to improving the quality of education and of life. Our classrooms should change year after year as we learn.

Could I adapt the model of the supper table of my youth to the classroom? Certainly I could try. During twenty years of teaching in public schools in Washington Heights, New York City, that was my goal. We had mandated basal readers and workbooks and endless tests, but even under those conditions there were ways to work toward that goal. There *are* ways to bring inquiry-based multicultural education into most schools. I hope this book will help educators and families in mainstream and alternative schools to do so.

My last four years of teaching have been at Manhattan New School, an alternative public elementary school in New York City. Many of its classrooms have the artifacts of a home—sofas, lamps, carpets, pets, an abundance of books and pictures. Social studies work flows out of classrooms and into the halls. Even our kindergarten students study Spanish. Diversity is respected. Shelley Harwayne, the principal, believes in the children's right to an inquiry-based multicultural education. Because she respects us as educators, she encourages us to develop our own styles of teaching. She challenges us to question our own techniques, to observe other teachers and to be observed, to study and read, and to work always to improve the quality of our teaching.

My philosophy involves an immersion approach. Whatever your theme for study, immerse yourself and your class in it, live it, breathe it. If you are studying about your school community, bring the families, neighbors, shopkeepers, and long-time residents into the classroom. Go out to the homes and job sites. Take your journals there. Fill yourself and your students with poetry, stories, and songs of community life. Where is the math in the neighborhood—in the shapes of buildings, the designs in walls, the patterns in gates and bricks? Where is the science—plant and animal life, weather patterns? As old buildings go down and new ones rise, who are the workers who make this happen?

For a cultural study, immerse your class in the culture for weeks or months. Cook the foods. Taste the tastes. Sing the songs and hear the stories. Meet the people. Ask the questions.

Like many others, I'm concerned and worried about the quality of life in our world. I want my students to help, in big ways and small, to make this a better world. Over the years many of my students have moved from developing understanding and awareness to using their knowledge to bring about change. Social action can include talking to family and friends about an issue; writing letters; writing stories; songs, and poems; making signs; raising money for books for children in a developing country; painting murals; marching. I believe that social action is an essential aspect of the classroom experience.

Reading, writing, science, math, literature, the arts, and other curriculum areas are tools for learning and thinking about ourselves and the world. They are the infrastructure of our classroom. The content of our inquiry studies will drive the curriculum.

Interviews are the central focus of our inquiry studies. They are our major source of new information and concepts. The interview is seeable, hearable, touchable. It is right there in front of the children and teacher. Through our questions, discussions, role playing, and note taking, the children are part of the interview, making interviews a very active form of learning.

In areas such as literature and mathematics, children learn to think about patterns. In social studies, too, there are patterns: All people need food, clothing, and shelter; people have thoughts and feelings. Because there are many interviews and subsequent activities, children learn to see these common patterns of life.

During an interview, children may find things in common with their own lives or things that are quite different. This experience makes us feel part of the human family. We can enjoy the similarities and honor the differences.

Interviews are the starting point for this exploratory journey. We need the reading, writing, science, math, literature, and the arts not only to help process and understand the information from the interviews, but also to extend our learning further.

Chapter 1 walks us through an actual interview. Chapters 2 through 4 detail how to choose interview subjects, how to formulate questions and conduct interviews, and how to extend the learning from interviews via activities involving different curriculum areas. Chapter 5 outlines the daily schedule: Reading and Research Workshop; Math, Writing, and Science Workshops; Reading Time, Meeting Time, and Center Time, and shows how interviews fit into the daily schedule. Chapter 6 walks us through a year-long classroom study of People at Work, showing us how the learned concepts are kept alive after the interviews are over.

At the Supper Table—
A Tribute

My own training began at the supper table of my youth with my parents, Anne and Milton Rogovin. Supper was a ritual. Rousing discussions abounded. Our father, an avid reader and a social activist, loved to "take anyone on" in a discussion about politics. The war in Vietnam was an ongoing supper-time topic. Any guest would surely encounter a serious discussion.

Supper was so much more than food. Our father had his favorite poets, Bertolt Brecht, Langston Hughes, and Pablo Neruda. To teach us a lesson in history or philosophy, my father would often quote a poem. Here is one of his favorites (Brecht 1947, 109):

A WORKER READS HISTORY
Bertolt Brecht

Who built the seven gates of Thebes?
The books are filled with names of kings.
Was it kings who hauled the craggy blocks of stone?
And Babylon, so many times destroyed,
Who built the city up each time? In which of Lima's
 houses,
That city glittering with gold, lived those who built it?
In the evening when the Chinese wall was finished
Where did the masons go? Imperial Rome
Is full of arcs of triumph. Who reared them up? Over
 whom

Did the Caesars triumph? Byzantium lives in song,
Were all her dwellings palaces? And even in Atlantis of the
    legend
The night the sea rushed in,
The drowning men still bellowed for their slaves.

Young Alexander conquered India.
He alone?
Caesar beat the Gauls.
Was there not even a cook in his army?
Philip of Spain wept as his fleet
Was sunk and destroyed. Were there no other tears?
Frederick the Great triumphed in the Seven Years War.
   Who
Triumphed with him?

Each page a victory,
At whose expense the victory ball?
Every ten years a great man,
Who paid the piper?

So many particulars.
So many questions.

Poetry seems to be my father's way of expressing his values. Bertolt Brecht's poem reverberates in my mind. It's not just famous people who are the heroes. Each family, each block, each community organization, each school, each town and city has its driving forces, its heroes and heroines. I want to bring that supper table into my class-room.

Neighborhoods in Buffalo were segregated at the time of my childhood. So were most of the schools. The curriculum was Eurocentric. At the supper table my father read newspaper articles and quotes from books—offering vastly different viewpoints from those we heard at school.

At the supper table we talked about our Saturday classes at the science museum. Our parents took us there regularly, partly because they wanted us to love science and partly because it was an interracial program. Later I enrolled in programs at the YWCA, where again I would be with children of many races and nationalities. This was my parents' way of combating the segregation in the society around us. I want our classrooms to bring people of various races and nationalities together.

Of course, my sister, Ellen, and my brother, Mark, and I had the usual sibling issues that had to be worked out. Who took my candy? Who would shovel the snow? The day-to-day conflicts of childhood were brought to the supper table also.

Our mother taught special education. At the supper table we heard about the tribulations of her students. She talked about her efforts to get other children to stop making fun of the students in her special education classes. I want to bring that tolerance and understanding of people with special needs into my classroom.

After discussing family matters, we looked at an ever-changing art exhibit on display on a bulletin board at the end of our kitchen table. We came to appreciate Vincent Van Gogh, Käthe Kollwitz, Paul Gauguin, Pablo Picasso, Mexican muralists, nature scenes by Chinese artists, and sculptures by African artists. Our mother went to the public library each week for more art books. Between bites of food, we looked at them and talked about them.

Our father, now eighty-seven years old, worked as an optometrist. But his real love was photography. He photographed "the forgotten ones," the people of Bertolt Brecht's poems—the men and women who worked in the steel mills of Buffalo, the coal mines of West Virginia, Mexico, Scotland, Germany, Spain, and Zimbabwe. Over a twenty-year period he took photo after photo on six square blocks of the Lower West Side of Buffalo, a poor neighborhood with residents from many ethnic groups. We were his critics. And we heard the stories behind the photographs. I want my students to find ways to express themselves through the arts and to treasure the art of others.

Our parents modeled social activism as they marched against the war in Vietnam or helped my brother and other young men resist the draft. Our father modeled his belief that workers should receive decent wages and benefits by organizing optical workers, even though that was considered by some at the time to be un-American. He considered his social documentary photography a quieter form of social activism. And so he was called up by the House Un-American Activities Committee in the 1950s along with many other social activists. Our parents modeled a lifelong lesson for us when they refused to be silenced, when they refused to stop their activism. I want to bring that sense of justice, determination, and social activism into my classroom.

Listen in on an Interview

1

There is no formula for the perfect classroom interview. Your topics of study, your particular group of children and families, and your resources will differ from mine. These factors differ in my own classes from year to year. Your students may be aged five or eight or twelve. Just as we can't be skilled teachers of reading or writing the first year we enter a classroom, it takes time to develop the strategies and skills for conducting interviews in an inquiry-based classroom. Each year I find that I become more skilled at conducting interviews and turning the content of our interviews into our curriculum.

It is the beginning of first grade. We are already engaged in a year-long cultural study of the families in our class at Manhattan New School. This is our second interview. We are interviewing Beatrice, Tatiana's mother.

An Interview with Tatiana's Mother, Beatrice
It is nine o'clock on a September morning. The children sit on the carpet, their steno book interview journals in hand. Tatiana's mother, perhaps a little nervous, sits in the rocking chair, and I sit on a straight chair next to her. We welcome Beatrice to our classroom with a "Good morning." I ask if she remembers a lullaby her mother had sung to her, and soon she is singing a lullaby to us in Spanish. Tatiana, Kathy, and Alejandra already know the song from home and sing along with Beatrice.

When Beatrice tells us that Puerto Rico is an island, my first graders are prepared. I ask them, "Who can remind us what is an island?" Rosie responds, "It's land growing out of the water." There are other definitions, too. We had already interviewed a parent from Cuba the first week of school. We had looked at our school map and seen that Cuba is land surrounded by water. Now we look again at Cuba on the large map hanging on the wall behind us.

Earlier that week, during Meeting Time—a part of our daily schedule—we had recited poems from the book *Not a Copper Penny in Me House* (1993) by the Jamaican-born poet Monica Gunning. When I first introduced that book, we found the island of Jamaica on the map. It, too, was surrounded by water. We look again now at Jamaica on the map.

During Reading and Research Workshop—another period in our daily schedule—we have lots of maps accessible to the children. Some children had observed that Manhattan New School is also on an island and had shared that information with the class. Those earlier map activities and their own family experiences prepared the children for this interview with Beatrice. The children feel empowered when I bring their prior knowledge to the surface rather than just telling them the definition of *island*.

Beatrice points out Puerto Rico on the map. I ask, "How can we show in our interview journals that Puerto Rico is an island?" Elizabeth suggests that we draw some land with water all around it. Michelle suggests that we write the letter *I*. Amanda, who had started writing in kindergarten, says we can write *i*, *l*, and *d*.

I comment that each way of showing that Puerto Rico is an island is great. The children beam when I express my approval of each of their methods of recording the information Beatrice is sharing with us. I say, "Hold up your interview journal so we can all see how you showed that Puerto Rico is an island."

Alexandra asks Beatrice what animals live in Puerto Rico. When Beatrice says there are cows on the farms in Puerto Rico, I stop her and ask the children how we can show this in our journals. Kathy says, "We can draw a picture of a cow." Sheila suggests, "We can write the letter *c*." No one offers the entire word *cow*, but that's fine. It is only September of first grade.

Beatrice tells us about the cows, horses, chickens, and donkeys. After each of these, I stop her, repeat the name of the animal, and give the children an opportunity to take notes.

Beatrice tells us about the *coqui*, a tiny frog seen only in Puerto

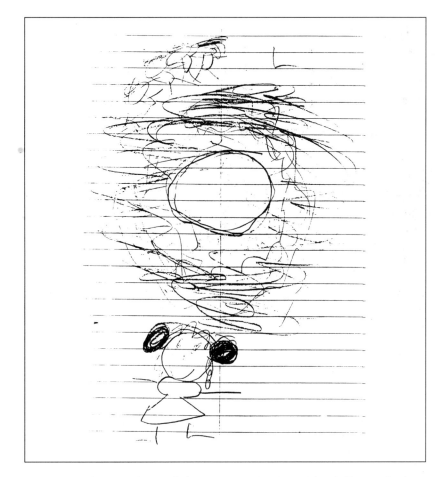

Lia's journal entry showing that Puerto Rico is an island (September).

Rico. I ask her if she knows the folksong "El Coqui." She does. We sing "El Coqui." I strum my guitar while Beatrice and I sing the verses and the children the chorus.

I suggest that someone ask Beatrice about the fruits and vegetables in Puerto Rico. Beatrice mentions mangoes, *guayavas*, avocados, *limonsitos*, and plantains. Some children have never heard of these foods. I assure them that we will eat some of these foods soon.

In a sense, as the teacher, I serve as interpreter and editor in this interview, stopping Beatrice to make sure that children understand the information she is presenting, selecting concepts for special emphasis, helping children to interact, and helping them record information.

Beatrice tells us next about the terrible drought in Puerto Rico. Hoping to draw from prior knowledge, I ask the children, "What is a drought?" But they don't know. We take time for a short science lesson about droughts. Beatrice tells us how the drought is affecting the people and the farm animals in Puerto Rico.

Then I say, "I wonder what the people in Puerto Rico can do to get enough water. Talk to the person next to you and think of ways to solve this problem." These one-to-one discussions are my way of democratizing classroom participation. In a small group each child has an opportunity to participate in the thinking and discussion. It slows down the process and enables more children to feel comfortable when we have whole-class discussions. Then gently I say, "Stop." This is the signal to end small-group discussions.

Clive says, "If Puerto Rico is an island, why can't they just take the water from the ocean and drink it or give it to the animals?" Michelle suggests they could bring some water from where we live. Of course, as the teacher, I have to make a choice. Do I explain the difficulties of desalinizing ocean water now? Do I promise more discussion of this another day so we can get on with the interview or so I can be better prepared? Or do I just drop the subject?

After a brief discussion about the drought, I ask the children how we could write in our journals about it. There are many suggestions. Then the children write in their journals. I tell them that we will return to the topic of drought another day. Later that day, I discuss with the science teacher how best to develop this topic. We will coordinate our efforts.

Now a major and controversial issue comes up. Beatrice tells us that a long time ago Columbus went to Puerto Rico and took it over for Spain. That's a big topic for young people. They have heard about Columbus before but never in this context. I decide to have the children do a role play about this. I direct most of the children to pretend they are Taino Indians who lived long ago in Puerto Rico. I whisper to the remaining group of children to be Columbus and his men and to get off their ship, kiss the ground, and say, "This land is for Spain now."

After the role play, I tell the children to talk about this with the person next to them. The children talk in groups of two or three. There are some rather animated discussions. I overhear one child ex-

Jhordan's journal entry showing the drought in Puerto Rico (September).

claim, "That wasn't nice. That was greedy." Another says, "That's okay. I don't mind."

We have a lively whole-class discussion about this. Then I promise to return to this topic another day. The concept of one country's taking over another will certainly come up at quite a few interviews during the year. Most young people are quite concerned about such issues of justice and injustice, of right and wrong, so this topic will surely be of interest to them.

There's so much more to learn from Beatrice about Puerto Rico.

But we have already touched on a few big issues. That's plenty for a September interview.

"Does anyone have something they want to say to Beatrice before we end the interview?" I ask. Elizabeth thanks Beatrice for singing the lullaby. At nearly every interview after that Elizabeth will ask the person to sing a lullaby. Lia thanks Beatrice for teaching us so much. Someone else tries to ask another question, but I remind him that we have finished asking questions for now. He says he liked the part where she talked about Columbus. I say, "Let's all say thank you to Beatrice." We do. The interview is over.

It's Snack Time. Beatrice had baked a typical cake of Puerto Rico and brought it in to share with us. It is delicious.

Keeping the Concepts Alive After the Interview

A half hour is just enough time for a September interview. There are many possibilities for taking concepts and issues from the interview and developing them further. As teachers, we need to rethink each interview. Which concepts from the interview are important? Which should be extended beyond the interview? How can we develop these concepts and issues through the various curriculum areas? Which could be developed at the daily Math Workshop? How can we introduce more connections to literature and music? Are there any topics for Science Workshop? Which concepts might be of interest to certain children? What materials will we need?

After the interview with Beatrice, I do that rethinking. This particular interview was rich with content. A student teacher and I make a chart indicating the grade-appropriate possibilities for extending the interview into as many areas of the curriculum as possible, always keeping in mind the children's interests and our own. The concepts and information Beatrice shared with us from her life experience and her cultural heritage will be like the threads on the loom of our curriculum, the content for skills development and for critical thinking. And there is now a bond between family and school.

Writing Homemade Books

Our homemade book about Beatrice will be our second that year. We gather briefly on the carpet, and I ask the children to look at the notes in their interview journals. We talk about them. Then each child makes a page about something important remembered from the interview. So early in the school year, most of the children express themselves through pictures. The student teacher and I ask what each drawing is about and write down what the children say.

I notice a few children are making things up about Beatrice—Beatrice dressed up as a queen at her castle or Beatrice at the park. I discuss this with them quietly, give them new paper, and help them think of something we actually heard at the interview. It will take a while for some children to learn to focus on the interview when they write a page for the homemade book. I know that by the time of the interview scheduled for next week, we won't need to take dictation. Everyone will write their page using invented spelling.

Reading

Shortly after the children finish their pages about Beatrice, we gather at Story Circle to hear our new homemade story. They can't wait to hear their own pages. They wiggle with excitement when I read them. Later in the school year we will bypass this step.

Since I want to use this homemade book for guided reading, I take the pages home and, using a felt-tipped pen, "translate" any invented spelling into standard English. Then I organize and number the pages. A parent volunteer makes a copy of *Beatrice, You Are Great!* for each child. Two weeks later the book is ready, and we begin using it to develop strategies for independent reading.

One strategy is prediction. Before we open the book, I ask the children to think about what we might find in a book about Beatrice. Clive thinks we will read about the drought, so I write *drought* on the dry-mark board. Michelle thinks we will read about how the horses and other animals didn't have enough water. I write *water* and *horses* on the board. Anticipating these words will make reading them easier.

Rashad remembers how thirsty the animals were, so I write *thirsty* on the board. I tell the children that when they see a word beginning with *th* like *thirsty*, they can stick their tongues out at me, they have my permission. They laugh. When we open the books a few minutes later, the children, most of whom are just beginning to read, are thrilled to find these *th* words.

I love to find ways to make phonics flow directly from our homemade books and other literature. It seems to make a lasting impression. During the week we will take that *th* from our book about Beatrice and begin a search for *th* words in the world around us—in other books, in newspapers, and in signs. Phonics is one aspect of whole language teaching—yet another way into the world of reading.

The children then work with the person next to them at Story

Circle, looking for those words we had predicted we would find in *Beatrice, You Are Great!* Clive finds the words *water* and *horse* on the page he wrote. Rashad shouts to his reading partner, "Look, Andrew, the word *horse* is on your page!" And he circles the word with his pencil.

When we read *Beatrice, You Are Great!* the second day, we develop the strategy of using pictures clues. Then it's usually easy for the child to guess the content of the writing. "Look, my page is in the book!" I hear Alexandra say to her partner, Michelle. With joy, she reads every word on the page. It's easy, because the picture reminded her of what she had dictated to the student teacher.

For my first twenty years of teaching in New York City public schools, I had been required to use basal readers. I never saw the children so excited or joyful when they read from a basal reader. Our homemade story is of the children, by the children, and for the children. Because they know the context and the content from the interview with Beatrice, they have a tremendous advantage as readers—they can use that information as a strategy for reading.

My goal at this time in the year is not only to develop strategies for children to become independent readers but also to make them feel comfortable reading.

In *Family Homework*, a weekly bulletin about our class that I send home (see Chapter 3), I tell the families that this book will be coming home. I encourage them to read it with their child and then sign it so that I know they have read it together. After two days of reading *Beatrice, You Are Great!* in class, the children take their books home. After I have seen the family signature, I send the book back home to become part of a homemade book library.

When we have the family celebration in November, at the end of our study of families from the Caribbean Islands and Central America, I say, "I want you to meet the famous Beatrice from our storybook." The families feel as if they know her already.

Writing

During the daily Writing Workshop, the children write stories, nonfiction, and poems about some of the topics from the interview with Beatrice, which they have researched further. These are writings about droughts around the world, about Columbus, about farm animals from the Caribbean, and about islands.

Science and Mural Making

The notes we took about farm animals serve a useful purpose. The day after the interview, several children refer to these notes. At Center

Tatiana's mother, Beatrice.

Time, another period in our daily schedule, they decide to paint a mural of a farm in Puerto Rico. The first day they paint the background, the blues of the sky and the greens of the grasses. They go back to their interview journals to recall which animals are on farms in Puerto Rico. They crayon in and then paint cows, horses, chickens, and donkeys.

Over the following weeks, after other interviews, we add more animals one could find at a typical Caribbean farm. Some children paint pigs, dogs, cats, goats, and sheep. Others color, cut, and glue pictures of animals onto the mural. They are able to show more details when they use crayons or markers.

Kathy loves animals. She gets so involved in our study that she finds photographs of some of the animals at home and brings them in. We glue them onto the mural.

Children in a research group work during Reading and Research Workshop to find out which other animals belong in our Caribbean farm mural. They look at pictures in storybooks and folktales from the Caribbean. They look in nonfiction books. I place tabs made from colorful tape in *National Geographic* magazines so they can look at articles about the Caribbean Islands. They record in their journals the animals they find. At Center Time, they add those animals to the mural. The children use invented spelling and make labels for each of the animals. I add the standard spelling below.

We move the six-by-four-foot mural from the painting area to a spot right near the classroom door. Whenever the children line up to leave the room, I can see them glancing at the mural or talking about it.

Science

Lisa, the science teacher, and I talk about how to pursue the subject of droughts. A group of researchers test Clive's idea of using ocean water. They make salt water and taste it. How can the salt be removed so people and animals can drink it? They experiment, unsuccessfully. I explain that this is a complicated process. Expensive machines are needed.

Other regions in the world are seriously affected by drought at this time. It is in the news. In *Family Homework* I ask families to be on the lookout for information about this topic. We read news articles and get reports from the TV news to find how the people are getting water for themselves and their animals. We find out that water is being shipped in to different areas in Puerto Rico. This is a great example of people helping people, of social action.

The children are beginning to learn about tools for their research. They are learning from Beatrice, from each other, from their families, from me, from newspapers, from TV. We will revisit the issue of drought all year long.

Math

Beatrice had introduced us to plantains, mangoes, avocados, and other foods from Puerto Rico. In *Family Homework* I ask the families to visit a supermarket or *bodega* during the next week to look at fruits and vegetables from the Caribbean Islands and Central America. Each child is asked to bring one fruit or vegetable from that region to school. Because so many family members work and probably cannot get to a market during the week, I suggest that the children bring the food either on Friday or on Monday. The children are excited when they arrive at school carrying *limonsitos*, plantains, bananas, pineapples, coconuts, pears, lemons, *guayavas*, mangoes, *papayas*, sugar cane, *yucas*, and more. Beatrice comes up to the room to help before she goes to her job. I had planned to work on sorting and attributes early in the year. Here was the perfect opportunity. We sit in a large circle around a large sheet of butcher paper. As we place the foods in the middle of the paper, we say the names of the foods. There is confusion over the different types of bananalike fruits. Beatrice straightens us out. Then I reorganize the foods, sorting them by color. I say, "Talk to the person next to you to see what I have done with the fruits and vegetables." The room is filled with lively conversations. Rosie says to her partner, "Look, Paula put big foods here and little foods here." Angela replies, "But look, here are little foods. It's not really a big and little sort." The two children go on to try to figure out how I had sorted the foods.

I listen to the conversations to get an idea of the thought processes and to watch how children are working together. Working together is not easy for some children at first. Some children wave their arms at me so I will call on them. They think they have the answer, and they want me to know that. But I want them to use their information to think with another child. I tell them to put their hands down for now.

Of course, while these discussions are going on, the children are practicing the names of the foods, teaching each other vocabulary, learning to listen, and bonding.

We return to our whole-class discussion of the foods. The children conclude that I sorted them by color. Again, I rearrange the foods in a pattern of large, small, large, small. We again have small-group and whole-class discussions.

After a few more times of my sorting the foods in different ways, it is their turn. A group of children decide how they will sort the foods, and the rest of us have to figure out how they sorted. All the children have an opportunity to sort. When we finish, I compliment them for being good teachers and working together so well. We will continue our work with sorting and attributes in the weeks ahead.

We will develop several math skills using these foods. We will count them by ones, twos, or fives. We will look at the shapes. We will add or subtract them. We will use pennies, nickels, and dimes to buy and sell the foods. We will make up word problems, using the names of children and foods.

Cooking

At Snack Time each day for the next week, we taste the fruits and vegetables, unfamiliar to many of the children. First we talk about appropriate ways to respond to food we don't like. Some children's reaction is, "Yuck!" or a horrible grimace. We discuss how this would feel to a child who loves this food or to the person who prepared it for us. "No, thank you" is a better way. Little by little, children become more open to new and different tastes.

Beatrice takes off from work later in the week to cook with us, our first school cooking experience that year. We make *platano maduro*, a very sweet fried plantain. As Beatrice talks, I write the recipe and instructions on a chart. We reread the recipe and then set to work. After washing hands, children wash, peel, and slice (with plastic knives) the *platanos*. Beatrice fries them over a hot plate.

There are lots of discussions. For example, children think the *platanos* look like bananas. We look at a picture of plantain and banana trees. We use all our senses to compare the fruits. The *platanos* taste sweeter than bananas. For all the children, and especially the second language learners in our class, this is a language-rich experience.

People walking by our classroom smell the *platanos* and come in to see what's cooking. We share the *platanos* with passersby and staff around the school. Sharing is an important part of our cooking experience. Not only is it a generous thing to do but also, while sharing, children have opportunities to teach others about *platanos*. It is empowering for them to teach the principal, the custodian, and students from other classes.

Trips

La Marqueta is a Caribbean market under the elevated tracks of the Long Island Rail Road at 115th Street and Park Avenue in New York City. I want to take the class to visit La Marqueta. It's a different experience than going with just your family. Rosie's mother, Susan, helps arrange for a school bus to the market a month after our interview with Beatrice. The market had been closed for renovations, so we couldn't go any earlier. The vendors, most of whom are from the

Caribbean Islands, give us a warm welcome. When we arrive at La Marqueta, the children already know a lot about the fruits and vegetables. Because of our classroom and homework experiences, they feel like experts. "Oh, there's a mango!" "Look at all the *platanos*!" "Look at that big pile of *yuca*!"

Several family members accompany us. Some are from the Caribbean Islands, others not. Beatrice and Alejandra's mother, Gabina, serve as interpreters and teachers. They know far more than I do about what we will see at La Marqueta. The vendors also serve as teachers.

Our first stop is the butcher shop, where they sell such items as pig ears, noses, and feet; cow tongues and hearts; and goat heads. Some children are making faces and saying "Yuck" at the strange foods. I say to Gabina and Beatrice, "I see that many children are saying 'Yuck' to the foods. Did you ever eat any of these foods?" Gabina tells us about roasting whole pigs and coconuts on the beach in the Dominican Republic. Other family members tell us about their experiences eating these foods. The vendor adds his stories. It's lucky for us that it's rather early in the morning and there aren't many customers.

I talk about how these are delicacies for many people from the Caribbean Islands and Central America. I ask how many children like to eat bacon. Many hands go up. "Which animal does bacon come from?" I ask. Many children don't know. A few say, "From a pig." "So you eat meat from a pig, too," I say.

"How many children like hamburgers?" I ask. That is a popular food. "Where does hamburger come from?" Some children know it is from cows. "So you eat cow meat, too. People from different places eat different parts of pigs and cows."

I suggest that we wouldn't want people to make fun of the foods we eat just because the foods are different from theirs. I ask the children not to make faces at the foods in the market. I had divided the children into small groups, each with an adult, and I ask each group to discuss this issue. When the student teacher first saw the meats in the butcher shop, she, too, had looked disgusted. Quietly, I talked to her about this. She hadn't realized that such a grimace sends a negative message to the children.

We move on, stopping to visit other shops at La Marqueta. The children are very polite and friendly. I have found that when you are friendly to vendors, they will take time to speak with the children and to teach them. The vendors shower us with gifts—fruits, candies, and even *pasteles* (meat pies made with green bananas called *guineos*).

The next day, each child makes a page about La Marqueta for a big book. I use a felt-tipped pen to translate the invented spelling into standard English. We keep the book in a large basket that is easily accessible to the children. Several parents had taken pictures. When the copies are ready, we post them on the bulletin board. Children make labels for each photograph.

Social Studies and Mural Making

At Center Time a group of children paint a mural map of Central America. We use a large sheet of butcher paper, about ten feet by four feet. The first day several children paint the ocean blues. The next day we do a whole-class map activity. I have drawn Cuba, Jamaica, and Puerto Rico on construction paper of different colors. The children label them and cut them out. We look at an atlas to figure out where to glue each island on our mural map. Then we make a key for the map.

As we interview the families from Central America, we will glue new countries on and add to the key, showing the country and which children in our class have families from that country. Our map experience is personalized. The children can associate real people with countries on the map. The children love to interpret the key for our mural map to anyone who comes into our classroom.

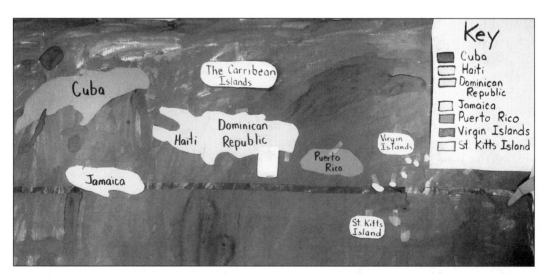

Mural map of the Caribbean Islands.

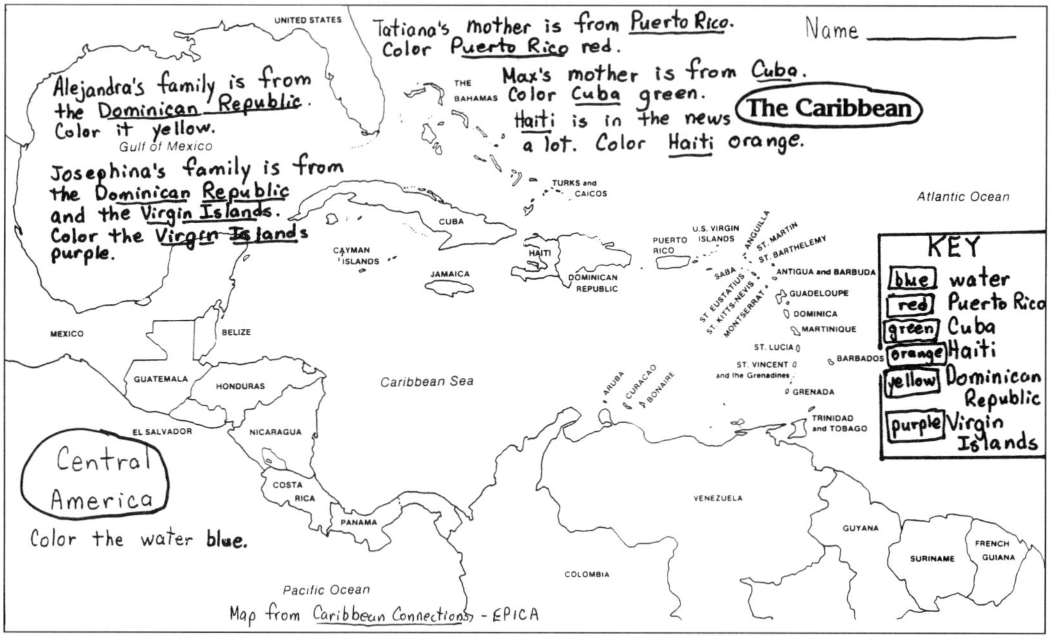
UNITED STATES
Tatiana's mother is from Puerto Rico. Color Puerto Rico red.
Name
Alejandra's family is from the Dominican Republic. Color it yellow.
Gulf of Mexico
THE BAHAMAS
Max's mother is from Cuba. Color Cuba green.
Haiti is in the news a lot. Color Haiti orange.
The Caribbean
Josephina's family is from the Dominican Republic and the Virgin Islands. Color the Virgin Islands purple.
TURKS and CAICOS
Atlantic Ocean
CUBA
CAYMAN ISLANDS
HAITI
DOMINICAN REPUBLIC
JAMAICA
PUERTO RICO
U.S. VIRGIN ISLANDS
ANGUILLA
ST. MARTIN
ST. BARTHELEMY
SABA
ST. EUSTATIUS
ST. KITTS-NEVIS
MONTSERRAT
ANTIGUA and BARBUDA
GUADELOUPE
DOMINICA
MARTINIQUE
ST. LUCIA
BARBADOS
ST. VINCENT and the Grenadines
GRENADA
TRINIDAD and TOBAGO
KEY
blue water
red Puerto Rico
green Cuba
orange Haiti
yellow Dominican Republic
purple Virgin Islands
MEXICO
BELIZE
GUATEMALA
HONDURAS
Caribbean Sea
ARUBA
CURACAO
BONAIRE
EL SALVADOR
NICARAGUA
Central America
COSTA RICA
PANAMA
VENEZUELA
GUYANA
SURINAME
FRENCH GUIANA
Color the water blue.
COLOMBIA
Pacific Ocean
Map from Caribbean Connections - EPICA

Excerpt from *Family Homework*.

Once the children take an active part in making a key on our map, they begin to notice and read keys on other maps. We will make keys of all sorts in the classroom.

This map work will become an integral part of the homework families do together. As children work on maps with their families, they will develop map skills such as making and interpreting keys, coloring contiguous countries different colors, seeing the relation of these countries to New York City.

My young students don't need to memorize names of countries. They seem to learn them by hearing them repeatedly when we read stories and poems from the region and conduct interviews, and when they are doing family homework or watching the news. They are aware of information provided by different kinds of maps, such as topography, climate, and products. I know from their responses and discussions that my students are getting a *sense* of the maps. We save the maps from the homework in an atlas. By the end of the year, each child will have an atlas to keep.

In the schoolyard parents tell me they are pleased to hear their six-year-olds talking about the different islands in the Caribbean. They say that when their children hear the names of those countries on the news, they perk up and listen. Perhaps these small experiences in school can stimulate a lifelong interest in current events.

Any map can be personalized by including the birthplace of class family members and friends, poets and authors, scientists and mathematicians, athletes, or artists from a region. A map assignment could look like this:

Tatiana's mother, Beatrice, is from Puerto Rico. Color Puerto Rico.

Jhordan's mother, Joan, is from St. Lucia. Color St. Lucia.

Alejandra's father, Angel, is from the Dominican Republic. Color the Dominican Republic.

Monica Gunning is from Jamaica. She wrote *Not a Copper Penny in Me House*. Color Jamaica.

Lynn Joseph is from Trinidad. She wrote *Coconut Kind of Day: Island Poems*. Color Trinidad.

Make each country a different color.

Color the water blue.

Sometimes I wonder what such young children think when they look at a map. Certainly they don't have a deep understanding of actual distances. Even after looking at a globe, they still don't really understand that the earth is round. Perhaps these are matters we need to touch on lightly in the earlier grades and then revisit in the third and fourth grades.

Drama

We return to the issue of Columbus the next week, role playing again the story Beatrice had told us. Drama is a useful tool for developing understanding of difficult and complex concepts. It is important that children have an opportunity to play different roles—sometimes being a Taino, sometimes being a representative of Columbus. That way they can develop critical thinking skills by examining different perspectives.

The same issue will surface again when we interview Jhordan's mother, Joan, who is from St. Lucia. She will tell us how people from both England and France took over the island of St. Lucia. A few months later Sheila's mother will tell a similar story, about how her country, Ireland, was taken over by England. Children will begin to recognize the pattern.

Music and Reading

A daily ritual in our classroom is Meeting Time, right after lunch. We add the songs from our interview with Beatrice to our repertoire. At lunchtime I printed the words on a chart so that the children can read the words as they sing. During our study of the Caribbean Islands and Central America we will learn many songs from the region.

The songs become a shared reading experience. In the songs we find sight words we know, such as *the*, *on*, *and*, *I*, and *stop*. I introduce new words. Looking for patterns or for rhyming words in the songs becomes another strategy for figuring out new words.

Sometimes phonetic elements or phonics issues become obvious as I look at the words from songs, and I consider the phonics strategies I can teach the children.

Before school one day, when I was writing the words for the song "Jamaica Farewell," by Irving Burgie, on a chart, I noticed several phrases with the letters *ou* and *ow*—*down the way*, *mountain top*, and *cry out*. I decided to seize the opportunity to practice the *ow* and *ou* sound.

"This word *down*," I say, as I point to the word on the chart, "has an *ow* in it." I tell a silly story about how *ow* and *ou* were out walking. They bumped into something and hurt their hands. They said, "*Ow, ou*"! I shake my hand as if I had hurt it. I tell the children that sometimes *ow* or *ou* says that sound. We shake our hands and practice saying, "*ow, ou*." We sing line by line through the song, stopping only when we find words with *ou* or *ow*. The children are quick to find the words *mountain*, *out*, *town*, and *around*.

"Does anyone remember one of the animals Beatrice told us about which has that same *ow* sound?" I ask. Several children call out, "Cow." We think of other *ou* and *ow* words like *town*, *clown*, *now*, *cow*, *our*, which I write on the dry-mark board. This sparks an interest in *ow*s and *ou*s that will last all year, giving the children access to many new words.

Then we return to our singing. We sing "Tingalayo," a West Indian folksong; "Guantanamera," a song (by José Fernandez Diaz, adapted by Pete Seeger and Julian Orban) from our first interview written to a poem by the Cuban poet José Marti; "Linstead Market," a

Jamaican folksong; and *"Day-O"* (by Eric Darling, Bob Carey, and Alan Arkin).

The Spanish teacher, Carmen, has taught the children several songs during Spanish class, and later she and the families will teach us Latin American songs from *Arroz Con Leche* (Delacre 1989).

Each song has a potential for word study experiences. Because we sing the songs each day, reading them is very comfortable for new readers. Sometimes I put copies of the songs into *Family Homework* for the children and families to sing and read together. When we have our celebration of the Caribbean Islands and Central America study, the families seem to know all the songs.

Poetry and Reading

Beatrice has sparked an interest in the Caribbean Islands and Central America. Each day at Meeting Time we read and recite poems from the region. Sometimes I write the poems on a chart and use them for shared reading. Because the children get so much pleasure from reciting the poems, they hardly realize they are working on their reading skills.

My class loves the poems in *Coconut Kind of Day* (1990), by the Trinidadian poet Lynn Joseph. Her poem "The Palet Man" has within it tremendous potential for developing reading skills and cultural awareness.

THE PALET MAN
Lynn Joseph

"Soursop, coconut, mango, lime!"
Neville, Arjune, Jasmine, and I
run down the street
to the palet man.
Count out our change
as we get in line,
Wait our turn
and *then* decide:
soursop, coconut, mango, or lime?

There are phonics concepts represented in words with *ou* and *ow* and in words with silent *e* at the end. There are quotation marks, lists with commas, and more. I can choose to focus on any of these topics. The children are thrilled to know that in Trinidad there are people who sell ices and ice cream on the street, just as in New York, Puerto

Rico, the Dominican Republic, and other countries represented by the families. In Trinidad the vendors are called palet men. We would find out later, through our research, that *soursop* is the same as *guanabana*. We would get to taste these tropical flavors in sorbets and in homemade milkshakes.

Assessing the Understanding

At the interview with Beatrice and during the activities flowing from it, I find many ways to assess the children's understanding. I look at the quality of participation during the interview and later discussions; the children's ability to develop a relevant page for our homemade book; and during guided reading, whether they use the information from the interview to predict what will be in our homemade book. I look at their comprehension skills. Are they using the information from the interview and research to write fiction, nonfiction, or poetry in Writing Workshop? Are they able to see the connections between math and interview topics? I observe as the skills develop. At Meeting Time, when we recite poetry, sing, or listen to a story, I watch the children participate. I listen for children to make connections between social studies issues and music, poetry, literature, or the other curriculum areas. At Center Time I get involved in the mural-making discussions so that I can hear the children's thoughts. I look at the small paintings, Plasticine objects, or crafts. I look at the *Family Homework* assignments related to the interview with Beatrice. Often family members will give me feedback about discussions at home. All these are part of the portfolio of assessment.

Children's Thoughts About the Interview

How does Tatiana feel after this interview? She is proud that her mother helped teach our class. Now her mother is also our teacher. Now everyone knows her mother's name. When they see Beatrice volunteering in the lunchroom a few days each week, the children go right over to her with questions and hugs.

When we publish our new book, *Beatrice, You Are Great!* Tatiana is thrilled. So are her parents. Tatiana hadn't known much about Puerto Rico. This interview has helped Tatiana's mother give her the gift of cultural identity.

Two years later, the PTA hired Beatrice to work in the lunchroom, and she subsequently became the assistant to the science teacher.

As for the other children in the class, they can't hear *Puerto Rico* on the news, in a story, in a book of poetry without a smile, without commenting, "I know about Puerto Rico." Their parents tell me this over and over. "Oh, Paula, we heard about Puerto Rico on the news last night, and Andrew rushed over to the TV to hear the story."

And so, inquiry is taking root—one question leads to another.

The Interview—Fulcrum of the Curriculum 2

What Is an Inquiry-Based Curriculum?

When children are young, they ask adults "Why?" all the time. They want to know, "What is this?" or "When will we get there?" Initially, some parents answer the questions, but then many tire of the endless questions. So often we hear parents, even some teachers, telling young children to stop asking so many questions. That's a shame, because it is that spirit of questioning that is the essence of inquiry and research.

I want my students to ask questions and more questions. Asking questions and then finding answers is for me an essential aspect of high-quality education. This approach applies to learning about anything. I want young children to think of themselves as researchers. I want them to thoughtfully examine the fabric of our society. Inquiry is at the center of our curriculum.

Some say that five- or six-year-olds are too young to become researchers. Research in early childhood is a notion rarely mentioned in colleges of education. But young children are researchers. It's their way of life. Certainly they can learn more formal ways to conduct research.

In *The Big Picture* (1993), Keith Pigdon and Marilyn Woolley discuss the concept of the inquiry model: "Inquiry approaches provide conditions which allow learners to take control of their learning, to build on their prior knowledge, to make and test predictions, to gather and organize information and to synthesize their findings.

These conditions encourage risk-taking, approximation, the exploration of patterns and relationships, reflection on experience, and an understanding of differing interests, points of view and value positions." (p. 16)

Interviews—Our Primary Research Tool

Over the course of the year my students learn how to use many different resources to find answers to their questions. They conduct a tremendous amount of research. Because I want the reader to see the context of the interviews, I have included in this chapter information about research in my classroom. The focus of this book is the use of interviews as a primary research tool.

Interviews are inquiry. Interviews are the fulcrum of our inquiry-based curriculum. Interviews are the tool we use to learn from and about each person. Interviews are the young people's version of oral history, a research tool used in some high schools and colleges as well.

In each person are stories, songs and dances, joys and hardships, rituals and customs, skills and talents, life experiences, varying degrees of formal education, special recipes, and opinions that constitute the individual's history and culture. The children, their families, friends, and neighbors, members of our school community, and workers are the primary sources of information for our research. What we can learn from interviews is often far beyond the reach of any textbook.

We don't know much about people until we ask questions. A security guard we greet each morning as we enter school may be a hero of the civil rights struggle in the 1960s. The mother of a student's friend may be a skilled seamstress. The woman with the hard hat at the construction site may be an electrician. The mother of a friend from dance class may be the teacher from the school for the deaf who will explain how coaches help some deaf people get jobs. The eighty-one-year-old woman sitting next to Elliot at church may be the granddaughter of a famous inventor. The friend of a child's grandmother may be the person we were looking for to explain how to make artificial flowers. The man who quietly brings his daughter to school every day may work at the grocery store and know how to cut sugar cane for a snack or how to sing a gentle lullaby.

Interviews, an Opportunity to Build Self-awareness and Self-esteem

Interviews give children an opportunity to build self-awareness and self-esteem. At a forum in Teaneck, New Jersey, called "A Conversation Devoted to the Reduction of Bias," on May 14, 1996, Dr.

Peggy McIntosh stated, "All students and all people have stories . . . Children need to find themselves in history. Children need to be invited to make textbooks of their lives . . . Curriculum must take all children seriously." When I heard Dr. McIntosh say this, I smiled. It felt to me as if she were helping me summarize my philosophy of education. At the same forum, Gil Noble, the producer, creator, and host of WABC-TV's *Like It Is*, talked about the importance of bringing children and their histories into the curriculum, the textbooks, and the mass media. He said, "The more I learned about my history, the more it squared my shoulders."

At the beginning of the school year, my students walk into the classroom bringing a multitude of histories. Some have home lives filled with history and culture. Others come from families with little awareness of their roots. They are the descendants of coal miners, now displaced and moved to large cities. They are from families forced away from their homes in Africa long ago, now migrated to New York. Some have fled the war in Bosnia. The hope for a better life drew others. My students are the children of building superintendents, writers, hospital workers, teachers, sanitation workers, lawyers, garment workers, and hotel housekeepers. There are parents who work two jobs and those who work long past their children's bedtimes; some with no financial worries and some who are unemployed.

It's the fabric made of many histories woven together that supports inclusive and content-rich learning. Examining and appreciating the cloth of many stories is my first-grade curriculum. Learning about diversity can be a great joy—the joy of self-awareness and the joy of understanding and appreciating others. When we study diversity, we find common threads. The study called inquiry-based multicultural education can bring about greater tolerance in a world filled with intolerance and prejudice.

An interview is a gift—the gift of one's cultural identity and the gift of self-esteem. For those children who are unfamiliar with their background, the classroom interview may be the introduction to their own family's history and culture.

Taking a family member out of the home setting and bringing him into the spotlight at a classroom interview can actually shift how a child views that person. Children often have no idea what their parents do at work, or what work their grandparents do or did. Often, through the interview, children develop new respect for members of their family.

As we interviewed Lee's mother, Crescenciana, I watched Lee. Crescenciana was teaching us about her work as a child laborer and then a garment worker. She was communicating with us using the English Lee had taught her. Lee was beaming.

A smile lit up Nigel's face when we interviewed his mother, Pauline. Pauline told us about her work as a former day care teacher. She can no longer work because of a problem with her spine, and through the interview with Pauline the children learned about disabilities. This interview sparked a year-long study of disabilities during our research about People at Work. We talked about how important it is for government to help people with disabilities and about how people got laws passed to protect the right of the disabled to work.

The two sisters, Almedina and Melisa, had probably never thought of their mother, Esma, as someone who would teach their classmates. Their father had died when they were babies. At her interview, Esma's jobs as a single parent and a building superintendent were elevated to great importance in our classroom. How wonderful that must have felt to Almedina and Melisa.

Vicky's mother, Milagros, had converted to a different religion when she married. She had set aside her Puerto Rican heritage. For Vicky, the interview was a gift of the music and literature, the history and customs, and the language of Puerto Rico.

Amanda's father, Hugh, is a Cherokee Indian and had already taught her about her heritage. Hugh was quite willing to come for an interview. However, her mother, Linda, was hesitant to be interviewed because she wasn't very familiar with her own cultural heritage. Her family was from Scotland, Ireland, and England. Amanda was so persistent, that she and Linda decided to do some research at home so they would be ready for an interview. They would focus on Linda's Scottish heritage. On the day of the interview Linda came dressed in a Scottish plaid suit. She brought a tie with the plaid of her Ross family clan and a kilt. Linda and Amanda taught us to dance to the folksong "Did You Ever See a Lassie?" Amanda brought three library books about Scotland, and they had baked Scottish soda bread for snack.

What Is the Context for Our Interviews?
I want the children to think of themselves as researchers and inquirers. The interviews are a major component of our inquiry studies. Our inquiry studies focus on a social studies theme.

Research in an Inquiry-Based Classroom
Research is

wondering about the world
starting from what you know and asking questions
thinking about the many ways you can find answers
seeking out those ways to find answers
making guesses or hypotheses
observing, reading, listening, experimenting, and thinking
drawing conclusions
undoing misinformation and stereotypes
sharing with other people
using our information to help to improve our society

Selecting a Theme for an Inquiry-Based Curriculum
Several factors influence the selection of a topic for a thematic study.

*The requirements and standards of a particular school, the local board of
education, or the State Board of Education.* Most school systems have
curriculum standards or guidelines. The New York City Board of Education's *Curriculum Frameworks* (1995) is inquiry-based and multicultural in essence. The topics and goals for social studies in early
childhood classes are very broad: "self/family/community."

These are a few of the expected outcomes from *Curriculum
Frameworks*:

Students will

- Demonstrate an appreciation of self, as well as the
  diversity of others in their school, community, and
  around the nation

- Understand that each individual has needs, desires, and
  abilities that are influenced by environment and culture

- Appreciate that families follow different traditions and
  customs

- Examine some of the ways people in communities earn
  a living to help meet their needs and wants

- Understand that most people around the nation live in
  families or family-like groups, and that family members
  are interdependent and play different roles at different
  times (p. 173).

Fortunately, at Manhattan New School, teachers have the opportunity to develop their own plans of work within that very broad framework. Under that big umbrella of expected outcomes, there are many possibilities for thematic studies.

Sometimes school districts have extremely restrictive curriculum requirements. This was the case in the schools where I taught for my first twenty years. Despite these restrictions, I was able to develop an inquiry-based curriculum. I used to think of what I did there as "stretching it." For example, if the official requirement was to teach about the nuclear family, I would meet that requirement. Then I would stretch the topic, and we would inquire about families of different shapes, sizes, and cultures. We were required to teach about Columbus discovering America. I stretched that topic so that my students could examine other perspectives about this issue. When the required topic was "People live in different kinds of houses," I stretched the topic so that we could learn more about homelessness.

The range of topics, issues, and concepts that could arise during interviews, trips, and extended activities. Within the theme there must be plenty of opportunities for extension into age-appropriate research and for critical thinking, reading, math, writing, science, art, drama, and other curriculum areas.

Finding an appropriate topic is not always easy. Some kindergarten teachers decided to do a year-long inquiry study about bread. After a few months, they found that the topic wasn't broad enough and the children and teachers were losing interest. That was fine. They moved on to something else. One year I decided to focus for the first two months of school on a study of People at Work. I realized very quickly that I couldn't possibly end this study in October. I dropped my other plans, and we stayed with this topic until the end of June.

My first- and second-grade classes in the past have been involved in these studies:

Our School Neighborhood

Our Block

Native American History and Culture

*We're All One Family Under the Sky—Our Class Families'
Cultures and Histories* (adapted from the song "Under One
Sky," by folksinger Ruth Pelham—see Blood and Patterson
1992)

Construction Sites

People at Work

Usually our thematic study lasts one school year. Sometimes we have a year-long theme that is "chunked." For example, for the year-long theme We're All One Family Under the Sky, we divided the year into four chunks: a few months for the study of our families from the Caribbean Islands and Central America, a few months for the study of our families from Europe, a few months for the study of our families of African background, and one month for the study of a Cherokee Indian family.

Suppose you are considering a thematic study about food. All children have had some experiences with food and where it is bought. This theme is immediate, relevant, and generative.

Some questions you might ask are: Where does our food come from? How is our food transported to the stores? Who produces our food? What foods are eaten in other countries or by people of different cultures? How does the soil or water supply determine the foods people eat? There are certainly enough issues for a thematic study.

There are possibilities for trips and interviews. Children can visit food stores: supermarkets, grocery stores, green markets, and wholesale markets. They can visit places where food is made or processed: bakeries, fast-food kitchens, canning factories, and meatpacking plants. They can visit places where food is grown or caught: farms, orchards, and fish hatcheries.

The class can interview a variety of food workers, family members whose jobs are connected with food workers, at school or at job sites. It's possible in some regions to interview farm workers and learn about their lives.

Can this topic sustain ongoing research groups? Children in research groups may want to trace a particular food from its origin to the supper table. They can examine labels on boxes and cans of food, and find the origins of the food on maps. And the cooking activities are limitless.

There is the issue of hunger, of children around the world or perhaps even in the school community who suffer from hunger and malnutrition. Possibilities for social action abound.

Within this broad topic of food, you can think of something that would pique the interest of every child. This could be a year-long thematic study, or you could narrow the focus and have the study last only a few months.

The time available for the study. In a school with many restrictions, the parameters for the thematic study will be limited. When I worked in schools where I was burdened with many pull-out programs, basal readers, pacing calendars, workbooks, and tests, I could not plan and develop a major thematic study. Instead, I limited the goals and integrated the thematic study into the curriculum as much as possible.

At Manhattan New School, there are few limitations on the time available for a thematic study. Because the thematic study is interdisciplinary, the scope and depth of the study can be extensive.

The teacher's interests. It's helpful to choose something that interests you. If you have little interest in a topic, I suggest trying to find a different theme. I want to be excited about our inquiry study. I, too, have to live with and work on the topic for a whole year.

The children's interests. Like adults, children tend to get more involved when they have an interest in a thematic study. If the topic is too narrow, it's more difficult for some children to get involved. When we think about a topic, we should consider whether there is room within that topic for a multitude of interests of our students. I try to find out about children's interests from kindergarten teachers, from the families, and from the children themselves.

For example, if a child is particularly interested in dance, I look for ways to incorporate that interest. In both cultural and job studies, that child can do research about dance and dancers. Perhaps that child's interest in dance will move other children to get involved.

If a child is particularly interested in science, I look for ways to incorporate that interest. When my class was doing research about People at Work, Daniel wasn't terribly interested in our thematic study until I found a way to incorporate his passion for rain forests. We formed a research group about rain forest workers. *Ranger Rick* magazine had an article about scientists who were documenting the plants and animals in rain forests so they could lobby the government to save certain regions. Luca's father, Elio, was in the room and overheard our discussion. The next morning Elio joined us and told us about some French scientists who are studying the rain forest from their workstation in a huge doughnutlike balloon in the canopy of the forest. Then, we invited Nico's father, Jorge, to speak about his brother's work as a documentary photographer in the Colombian rain forest. (Nico had been in my class three years before.) The researchers painted a mural about the rain forest. Daniel was thrilled.

Children's prior knowledge. Children who have had a great range of life experiences will bring them into a classroom study. They will become important resources in their research groups. The starting point for the research varies depending on the prior knowledge and experience of your students.

Children's attitudes. Attitudes play a big role for me when I think about the direction of our thematic studies. When I see that some of my students are particularly insensitive or hostile to people of other races, religions, or nationalities, or to people with disabilities, I try to bring these issues into our thematic study in the following ways:

- Select a theme that is broad enough to enable me to raise these issues.

- Schedule certain interviews early in the year so that a child will get to know adults of different races, religions, and nationalities. Many times I have seen friendships form after the barriers of fear are broken down during a classroom interview.

- Interview people with disabilities from our class families, the school community, or friends of the families. At the interviews, children will see a disabled person as a human being with feelings, talents, and concerns. They may come to respect how the person has struggled to deal with the disability.

- Select a comment at an interview for special emphasis. When Byron's father's college professor told him he should become a plumber instead of a writer, I knew that a role play and discussion of this would help shape values. When a child said that another child's mother wasn't as smart as the other parents because she didn't go to college, I took time to discuss this issue.

- Seek more resources and extend the time for a particular topic. Over the years I have had a few students whose families displayed overt forms of prejudice. One family told their child never to take food from a child of another racial background. Another family didn't want their child to associate outside of school with children of other races. Through our thematic studies I tried to counter such prejudice among the children.

Children's levels of skill. Academic skills are developmental. Any group of children can get involved in a thematic study. We just have to adjust the scope and the depth of the study to the children's levels of skill. I do an informal assessment of the children early in the year by speaking with families and previous teachers. Then I make my own observations. I continue to assess their skills throughout the year so that I will know how to proceed with our thematic study.

My motto has always been, "Never underestimate children." So many times I have taught children who had great difficulties in a previous grade. There may have been a number of reasons for this: problems at home, emotional problems, immaturity, learning disabilities, communication problems such as being unfamiliar with English in a monolingual class, or lack of interest. Children can and do change. When these same children get involved in a content-rich thematic study, many make a complete turnaround. Usually, when children are engaged in research, they become extremely motivated and improve their level of critical thinking.

Children's special needs.   We must always consider the special needs of children. For example, children who have difficulty focusing should have a less complex topic of study. You may want to schedule only a few interviews. Interviews will have to be shorter. There may be limitations on trips.

For a child who lacks self-esteem, you may want to work on research topics or schedule interviews that will bolster his self-esteem. For instance,

- Schedule some interviews with people of a similar ethnic background to the child.

- Interview families with different income levels or educational backgrounds. Children need to see that you value all families.

- Schedule interviews with families of children who lack self-esteem early in the school year.

- Work closely with the child or the family to learn about the child's special interests. Find a special place in the thematic study for those interests.

- Before or during the interview of that child's family member, try to identify something special that the child will feel proud of. For example, we interviewed Kathy's grandmother, Dora, who was devoting much of her time to taking care of her wheelchair-bound mother. We took time to discuss this, and after the interview, the children decided to name their homemade book *Dora Is So Nice.* This was a very important experience for Kathy.

The willingness of families to participate. The greater the family participation, the greater will be the resources for your thematic study. While it's great to have families who can come to help in the classroom, accommodating families with rigid work schedules or families with babies at home is just as important. I try to find opportunities for participation that will work for each family (see Chapter 3).

Available resources. It's critical to assess the availability of resources for a thematic study and to prepare adequate age-appropriate resources well in advance. During the school year, you can reach out to families and colleagues for additional resources. Suppose there are very few resources available for children who are not yet reading or who have limited reading skills. Perhaps family volunteers can work with the children in small groups. Perhaps children can help each other. But if you want the children to do some independent research, you may have to consider another topic with more appropriate resources.

Getting Started with the Thematic Study
I launch our inquiry study the first or second day of school. I want my students to be engaged in research right away. One school year is so short, and we have so much to do. The examples in this section, from thematic studies in my classes over the last four years, show the possibilities with different topics.

Building on students' prior knowledge. My assumption is that my students will know something about any major theme I introduce. Each child brings a different life experience into the classroom. A child who is struggling with reading or math may be the class "expert" on our inquiry topic. I build on prior knowledge. But I also examine that information. There may be misinformation or stereotypes.

One thematic study we did was People at Work. My students had been observing people at work for years. They might have stopped with a grownup at construction sites to see huge cranes lifting supplies to the tops of buildings. They might have said hello to the bus driver or the subway conductor. They might have watched the ice cream vendor scoop up their favorite ice cream. They might have watched sanitation workers lifting the garbage into their huge truck and perhaps wondered what happens to all that garbage.

My students knew a lot already as we approached our formal study of People at Work. We began our research by gathering on the carpet at story circle to discuss the many things they already knew about workers and jobs. As the research continued, other things they knew would arise.

Another year, when we did a study about Native American History and Culture, I began by asking the children what they knew about Indians. I cringed inside as I made a list of their "prior knowledge":

Indians wear feathers.
Indians kill children.
Indians fight.
Indians dance.
Indians live in tepees.
Indians use bows and arrows.
Indians do war whoops.

The list went on, filled with stereotypes and misconceptions. I accepted all information and wrote it down so that we could return to it as we learned to distinguish fact from fiction.

Asking questions. Next, we formulate questions about the topic of study, based on the interests of the children, the teacher, and the families.

The children's questions. If it is the first time children are involved in formulating questions for a study, their initial list of questions will usually be short. New questions will arise during the year and can be added to the list. During this process, it is important that the children know that

Any question is welcome.

Questions relating to a child's special interests (dolls, toys, sports, clothes, science) are encouraged.

Adults' questions are welcome.

No one will make fun of your question.

Once when my class did a study of the school neighborhood, Yorkville, the children's questions were:

Can we see the East River in Yorkville?
Who works here?
Who built the buildings?
Who made the buses, motorcycles, trains, and cars?
Who made us?
Who made the signs for the bus stops?
Where does the food in the stores come from?
Who makes the clothes in the stores?
Where do our books come from?
What kinds of trees are here?
Where do the horses come from? (referring to police horses)
Who made the furniture?
How did they make the floors, ceilings, and walls?

I smiled to myself at "Who made us?" What a huge question from a six-year-old. This was not appropriate for our community study, but it was sincere. I needed time to think about a response. At a later time, I told the children that this was an important question and that people have different ideas about it. They would learn what scientists have said when they were older. Or they could talk to their families about it. We dropped the topic and moved on.

In an inquiry-based classroom, children get better and better at asking questions. As they do research, children develop new interests. Their knowledge base builds. As the year goes on, their questions become more sophisticated and substantive.

When we launched our year-long People at Work study, I asked, "What would you like to know about jobs? Which jobs are particularly interesting to you?" I recorded their questions on a chart:

How do workers learn their jobs?

I want to know about dancers.

I want to know about people who do sports.

Who built the buildings in New York City?

Who works at Manhattan New School?

I want to know about musicians.

Who fixes the bridges?

Who works on our block?

How do they make fake flowers like the one Alina brought to school?

What jobs do our families do?

Why do some people have two or three jobs?

When our theme was We're All One Family Under the Sky, these were the questions as we launched the African-American chunk of the study in March:

> I want to know about dancers.
> I want to know about singers and musicians.
> What was slavery?
> How did slavery begin?
> How did slavery stop?
> I want to know about scientists.
> I want to know about construction workers.
> I want to know about authors.
> Are there popular foods like in the Caribbean Islands?
> I want to know about athletes.
> I want to know about civil rights workers. (added by Paula)

Some of these questions reflected the previous chunk of our study, about families from the Caribbean Islands and Central America. But the questions for the study of our families from Europe were very unusual for first graders. We launched that chunk of the study in May. Some of the questions for this topic were

> How do the people travel?
> Is there segregation?
> What kind of music do they have in Europe?
> What kinds of dances do people do in Europe?
> Do they play baseball, basketball, and football?
> What do people export from countries in Europe?
> Do they import things to Europe?

There were forty-two questions in all! The children became so enthusiastic that we had to stop from exhaustion. This was our final thematic chunk of the year. It was particularly interesting for me to see the questions about slavery and segregation coming from seven-year-olds. Clearly, their prior studies that year about Caribbean, Central American, and African-American culture and history had had a big impact on them. They had learned about slavery, segregation, discrimination, and other social justice issues, and they carried that learning into their new study about Europe.

During the course of a thematic study, I select only some of these questions to be the focus of our research and our interviews.

The teacher's questions.   While the children have their many questions, I also have mine. My questions reflect curriculum requirements from the school, the district, or the state. They also include my own particular concerns. There are general issues and understandings that should be developed over the course of the study. My particular questions and concerns for our People at Work study were

What jobs are done by members of our families?

What jobs do people do as parents?

What are some of the barriers to people's getting jobs—race, gender, and disability biases in our society?

How have people worked to overcome these barriers?

Which jobs used to exclude groups of people but are now inclusive? How did these changes come about?

What about people who do not have jobs?

What is child labor?

What are sweatshops, and what has been done or is being done to end sweatshops or bad working conditions?

Which jobs are public service jobs—teachers, sanitation workers, health department, firefighters, and so on?

During the time when the children are proposing their questions, I may suggest one or two of my own. But I know from experience that I will be able to bring up some of those additional topics during the course of the study. It's important for me to assess how children are doing before I introduce these more complex issues. Also, I want the initial list of questions to reflect primarily the children's interests.

The families' questions.   It's important that the families be aware of our inquiry-based thematic study and that they participate fully in the process. On the first day of school the families receive a copy of *Family Homework*, which describes our theme and invites their participation (see Chapter 3).

In September I invite families to an evening meeting in the classroom. Some schools call it Curriculum Night or Open House. We talk about our inquiry-based theme, and I show them the children's initial questions. Then I ask the families, "What are the questions you would want to ask if you were in the class?" One person takes notes, and I keep that list of questions in mind during the year. Certainly I will find ways to bring some of these questions into our research. I know from experience that if a family member is very interested in a topic, she will usually volunteer to help us with resources or actually help in class.

Returning to the questions. Periodically during the course of the thematic study, we look back at our list of questions. At the end of the study, the children and I return to our list of questions to assess which ones we have answered. Sometimes the children see that they have done lots of research. At other times they realize that they have only scratched the surface. We never even touched some of the other questions. I assure them that's okay. I say, "We are finished with our formal study of the Caribbean Islands and Central America. Does that mean we can't do any more research about it?" They laugh, and we discuss how this research can go on throughout their lives. New questions about the Caribbean Islands and Central America may always arise.

Searching for Answers

This is what makes our classroom so different from the classrooms of my youth. In our inquiry-based classroom, we locate and use a multitude of resources for our research.

Research tools. After complimenting the children for their questions, I ask them, "How will we find answers to these questions?" We make a list. If this the first year they have done formal thematic studies, or if this is the first study of the year, the list of resources will usually be quite short. Children might suggest looking at books, asking people, and looking at pictures.

By April or May, the children's list of resources for finding answers can be very long. Here is a list from our study We're All One Family Under the Sky:

> books
> nonfiction books
> folktales and stories

newspapers
magazines
encyclopedias
dictionaries
maps
atlases
interview relatives, friends, neighbors, others
videos
go on trips to museums and art galleries
go on trips to stores and markets, apartments, zoos
go to the library
travel to other countries
music—records, CDs, tapes
instruments
dance
movies
TV
radio
pictures
photographs
computers
food
clothes
toys
dolls
money
math
other languages

This May list is quite extraordinary for young children. How did they develop such a list of research resources?

Becoming conscious of how to get information. It is important that children become conscious of how they get information. During the course of the school year, each time a child finds information about our topic of study, I ask, "How did you get that information?" or "Where did you get that information?"

One time Alex told us that he got the information from his computer. Stephanie told us that she got her information from the man who works at the record store. Charlotte spoke to a neighbor. Albina and Almedina learned about different countries by examining the details in pictures in our poetry books day after day. Elliot found information on coins. Others saw specials on television.

We talk about how important it is to learn from our relatives. Once, during an interview, Sharice's mother, Sharon, told us that she planned to speak to her aunt in Alabama so that she could get more information about her family history. The children laughed to think that even our parents have to do research. Vickie, a paraprofessional at Manhattan New School, told us during an interview that she would have to go back to members of her family in Connecticut to get more information to answer the children's questions. Occasionally I ask children to practice learning from members of their family for a *Family Homework* assignment.

When a child discovers a new resource, I compliment the child, and we add that resource to our class list. This encourages children to think creatively about resources. Here is a list showing resources in different categories:

HUMAN RESOURCES	VISUAL AND AUDIOVISUAL MATERIALS	EXPERIENCES
family	books	cooking and sewing
peers	magazines	shopping
school staff	newspapers	arts and crafts
other people	encyclopedias	trips
	movies	block building
	videos	drama and role playing
	TV	singing
	computer	dancing
	records, tapes, CDs	sorting
		handling materials (clothes and objects from various cultures)

Once children see themselves as researchers, they look everywhere for information. Once they know they are in charge of finding the answers, they become bold and independent learners.

At a family meeting I asked the families how they would try to find answers, just as I asked the children. We talked about the fact that when most of us were children the encyclopedias, books, and textbooks were the standard sources of information. I pointed out that often teachers and parents spoon-feed answers or provide a single text with "the correct answers" because this is easier than challenging the children to search for other sources of information and other perspectives. Family members were pleased when we talked about encouraging that challenge and helping their young children learn to find and use both traditional and nontraditional research tools. Families frequently describe their children's enthusiasm about being researchers. Sometimes they find it difficult to walk home from school without their child stopping over and over to make observations, to read signs, to investigate, or to talk about what they did in class.

Breaking down stereotypes and misinformation. During our study of Native American History and Culture, when the children's prior knowledge reflected stereotypes and misinformation (see previous list about Indians), I saw that I had a huge job to do. I began, not by criticizing the children, but by saying, "Wow. You have a lot of information. Where did you get all that information about Indians?" We made a list:

> movies on TV
> movies and videos
> teachers
> family members
> friends
> pictures

"Did you know that sometimes our information is wrong?" I asked. Many children were astounded by my comment. I continued, "Some of the information you mentioned is not true. It's not your fault. Sometimes movies show the wrong information about Indians. For example, in some movies, Indians go around killing people with bows and arrows. It's not true that all Indians use bows and arrows. Long ago, many Indians did use bows and arrows for hunting. But they used lots of other tools for hunting, and today most Indians don't even hunt. They buy meat in stores like we do. And it's not true that Indians go around killing people. If we say that all Indians use bows and arrows or go around killing people, that is not true. It is a stereotype. Talk to the person next to you about this."

Sterotips are a cind of a lighe like if I wold say every Indian wacrs fethers that wold be a sterotip and you sterotips can't uoys it hers becuse peoples felings and if you told one you wold fele bad after you told it.

Page from Alexandra's book on stereotypes (April).

Stereotypes are a kind of a lie. Like if I would say every Indian wears feathers, that would be a stereotype. And you can't use stereotypes because it hurts people's feelings. And if you told one, you would feel bad after you told it.

There was a lively discussion. Then I said, "We can't always believe what we see in the movies. During the next few months, we'll try to find out what is a fact and what is a stereotype."

One year my first graders did research about Native American History and Culture for nearly two months. Then we watched different versions of the short segment in *Peter Pan* where Peter meets the Indians. The children sat, clipboards in hand, looking for stereotypes. In the Walt Disney version, the Indians did war whoops, wore feathers, danced around fires, and lived in tepees.

During the discussions afterward, the children were incensed. A father got the address of the CEO of the Disney Corporation. The children wrote to the CEO, appealing to him to make a new *Peter Pan* video without stereotypes about Indians. They never received an answer.

The children developed quite an advanced understanding of stereotypes. Now they were on the lookout for them. They extended their search far beyond our study of Native American History and Culture.

With older children, the concept of misinformation and stereotypes would be extended much further. One would work on checking multiple sources and challenging sources of information.

Acting on Our Knowledge

Each year I teach my children this poem from *The Dream Keeper and Other Poems* (1994) by Langston Hughes:

DREAMS

Hold fast to dreams
For if dreams die
Life is a broken-winged bird
That cannot fly.
Hold fast to dreams
For when dreams go
Life is a barren field
Frozen with snow.

My dream for my students is that from our inquiry studies they will develop a greater awareness and a better understanding of the world. Over the years I have encouraged them to use that knowledge to move beyond themselves to help others. Social activism can be as small an act as helping or sharing with a classmate. Even working cooperatively in a research group is a way to help oneself and others. Social activism can be community service in the classroom, school, or neighborhood. It may mean teaching other people about a social issue or problem, writing letters, presenting art, music, drama, or dance about a social issue, raising money for causes, or participating in walkathons or demonstrations.

Over the years all of the following projects evolved from inquiry-based studies in my classes:

- A group doing research about housing and homelessness in our community wrote to the mayor to ask what he was doing to help homeless people and to urge him to do more.

- After an interview with a father who ran a local soup kitchen and homeless shelter, our class organized a schoolwide collection of winter coats and cans of food.

- At an interview of several grandparents on our school's Grandparents' Day, we learned that all the grandfathers had been in World War II. We sang songs about peace. Then a group of children wrote to the President about peace. Several children painted a mural about Shel Silverstein's poem "Hug O'War," from the book *Where the Sidewalk Ends.* The mural was displayed in a hallway at school.

- During a two-month study about apartheid in South Africa, a group painted a mural about apartheid. The mural was displayed at a conference on apartheid and at the parade to welcome Nelson Mandela after his release from prison. My class worked with another class to raise over three hundred dollars at a bake sale for books for schools in South Africa.

- Children wrote poems about various social issues. These poems were published in a booklet at school and were shared with families and friends.

- My classes have presented plays about various issues at school and district programs.

Langston Hughes's poem resounds in my mind as I do my work as an educator. I know that our inquiry studies will make a difference.

Reaching out to the Community 3

Finding People to Interview

It is the families, the teacher, the children, and the community who are the threads of the loom, who create the warp and the weft of the fabric of our studies. People are our primary source of information. They know their cultures, their occupations, their histories in ways most books cannot convey.

Where, within and outside of the school, can we find people who will share information about their lives or work with the children? Where can we find people to help us answer questions from our thematic studies?

While I may have done some thematic studies more than once, no study has ever been the same. So each year I repeat the process. Each year there are new variables, new colors and textures of the threads—the interests and resources of the students and their families and of the teacher, the trips, the extension activities, and the ever-changing requirements of schools or boards of education.

Interviews with Family Members

First, I look among the extended families in our classroom for people to interview. Each family member is a potential resource for our classroom research:

parents   siblings
grandparents   cousins

43

aunts, uncles	stepsisters, stepbrothers
in-laws	step-grandparents
foster parents	godparents
stepparents	

Even family members who work are usually willing to take time to be interviewed. Rashad's grandmother, Virginia, arranged her classroom visit for a day she had to take off from work for a dental appointment. Suzannah's mother, Jean, rearranged some appointments at work so she could arrive late after the interview.

Some family members readily volunteer to be interviewed. Others are hesitant and need to be encouraged. I remember several occasions where I literally had to hold a parent's hands and walk him into the classroom for the interview. The people we interviewed always left our room after the interview smiling and relaxed.

Here are a few examples of what we can discover if we look for resources among the families represented in our classrooms.

Hispanic backgrounds. My classes at a school in Washington Heights, New York City, had approximately 92 percent of students from the Dominican Republic. We dedicated a lot of time to learning about Dominican history and culture. However, during the interviews, when we looked deeper, we learned that many of the families we had thought were Dominican had members from Puerto Rico, Cuba, Jamaica, Trinidad, and countries in South America and Asia. There were many bicultural families from the Caribbean Islands. We also interviewed the families from Asia and the Middle East and African-American families.

The families held a great variety of jobs. There were hospital workers, secretaries, storekeepers, security guards, subway workers, bank tellers, building superintendents, factory workers, and full-time mothers. Quite a few parents were students.

Though many of the stores in Washington Heights were owned by Hispanic merchants, others were not. For our neighborhood inquiry studies we interviewed people at the following places: grocery store, shoe store, beauty salon, a Chinese restaurant, Columbia-Presbyterian Hospital, and a senior citizens center we visited regularly.

African-American backgrounds. African-American students will have families from the Caribbean Islands and the West Indies, families recently from countries in Africa, families who left slavery only a few generations ago, families who arrived from the South to the big cities of the North during the Great Migration, and families who may have lived for generations in England or other British Commonwealth countries. You may have the African diaspora right there in your classroom. On several occasions, when we interviewed African-American families, we found that they had grandparents who were Native American.

European backgrounds.   Among the families of white students, there may be recent immigrants or long-time residents from Scandinavia, Central Europe, Eastern Europe, or British Commonwealth countries. Each family came to the United States for a different reason and at a different time in history. For example, there were families who left Ireland during the time of the Potato Famine. Although my classes at Manhattan New School are interracial, there are quite a few white children in them. The diversity of backgrounds is evident from the following list of family members we interviewed one year during the European chunk of We're All One Family Under the Sky:

Alexandra's father, Peter, whose family is from Italy

Alexandra's grandmother, born and raised in Italy

Amanda's mother, Linda, whose family is from Scotland, England, and Ireland

Andrew's father, Fred, whose parents were born in Italy

Andrew's grandfather, Raymond, whose parents were born and raised in Austria

Clive's father, Jonathan, born and raised in Liverpool, England

Iliana's mother, Maya, born and raised in Bulgaria

Lia's father, Anthony, whose parents were born and raised in Italy

Lia's grandmother, Laura, born and raised in Italy

Michelle's mother, Josephine, born and raised in Malta

Rosie's grandparents, Toni and Milton, born and raised in Germany

Shane's mother, Susan, whose family is from various countries in Europe

Shane's grandfather, Stanley, born in Germany

Sheila's mother, Mary, born and raised in Ireland

Shpen's mother, Sonia, born and raised in Yugoslavia and
Albania

Asian backgrounds. Stereotypes or lack of information sometimes
prevent us from seeing the diversity among Asian students. There
has been tremendous immigration from different countries in
Asia—Cambodia, Vietnam, Japan, China, and elsewhere. Families of
children who are Chinese may hail from Hong Kong, from different
provinces in China, or from families who settled temporarily in
other parts of the world. They will probably speak dialects of Chinese that sound quite different from each other. Each country or region has its own customs, history, music, stories, folktales, poetry,
and foods.

Different jobs. The interviews will reveal many different occupations
characteristic of the region where you teach. In some towns many of
the families work at the same factory or the same corporation, but
within that factory, mill, mine, hospital, or corporation people hold
different jobs.

Your class may have family members who do not work outside
the home or who have returned to school. Some adults may have
two or three jobs or do volunteer work. Others may be unemployed.

When Sheila was in my first-grade class, we interviewed her
mother, Mary. Mary had been a folk dancer and singer in Ireland.
Mary read an Irish folktale at the interview. She answered questions
about her country. Then she sang to us in Irish and in English. We
joined her in the choruses, flapping our arms like the farmer's chickens
and tapping our fists like the shoemakers' hammers. Then we danced.
Later that year, I invited Mary and Sheila to lead several classes in song
and dance on St. Patrick's Day.

The next year, when my class was doing research about Europe
during a cultural study, I invited Mary to come back for another interview. Later, when my class was doing research about People at Work,
we invited her back again to tell us about her former work as a folk
dancer and singer. Once more, we sang and danced. Then Mary told
us about her current work at the Irish Consulate. We role-played some
of the details of that job.

Interviews with People from the School

If your class has asked questions that cannot be answered at family interviews, or if your class lacks diversity, you can reach out beyond your class to interview people from your school like these:

children or families from other classes	custodians
paraprofessionals	secretaries
teachers	repair people
school aides	guidance staff
security guards	principals and assistant principals

John, the Manhattan New School custodian, wore Elvis T-shirts and belt buckles as he polished the floors of our ninety-five-year-old school. We interviewed him in the boiler room, where we saw the old coal shute and the newer gas boiler. Another day John came to the room to tell us about his father's job as a longshoreman. He came to our class several times to read stories, as he did with other classes.

We also interviewed Pauline, a school aide at Manhattan New School. Pauline did lunch duty and clerical work. When the children told her at lunch one day that we were learning about Italy, she asked if she could bake an Italian snack for them. I said yes, but only if she came for an interview about her parent's lives in Italy. Another year I invited Pauline to come back during our study of the community. The children wanted to know what it was like long ago in Yorkville. Pauline had lived in Yorkville all her life and had attended P.S. 190, now Manhattan New School. She told us about the men with horses and wagons who brought huge chunks of ice for the ice boxes. We learned about the shared bathrooms in the hallways of apartment buildings, the markets, and the old movie theaters. We learned that people of different nationalities couldn't live on the same block then—blocks were segregated. The children were surprised to hear about the desks in the old school, which were nailed to the floor, the ink wells, and the separate entrances for girls and boys. They wrote a homemade book about Pauline and painted a mural of our classroom long ago.

Interviews with People from Outside the School

If your school community lacks the diversity needed to answer your questions about different cultures, occupations, issues, or perspectives, you still have many options. With the help of the families and your colleagues, you can reach out to your town, city, or even further for people to interview. On several occasions, we have interviewed out-of-town guests, including my parents and friends, friends and relatives of students' families, friends and relatives of my colleagues, and guests visiting Manhattan New School from other cities and countries.

Among the friends and acquaintances of our class families, colleagues, and ourselves there is a gold mine of resources. As researchers we need to tap into those resources. Here are some places to look:

WORKERS IN PUBLIC SERVICE

letter carriers
firefighters
police officers
sanitation workers
librarians
teachers
bus, train, subway, trolley drivers
school bus drivers and matrons
health care and hospital
    workers

STUDENTS

high schools
colleges
vocational programs
graduate schools
adult education programs
foreign exchange students

OTHER RESOURCES

Yellow Pages
Reference room librarians
Internet and e-mail
Chambers of Commerce
Newspapers and magazines
Consulates and embassies

WORKERS AT OTHER PLACES

stores and markets
restaurants
recycling centers
museums and art galleries
theaters
farms (incl. migrant workers)
utility companies
shipping industries
factories
dairies
companies
zoos
mills
bridges and tunnels
labor unions

PROGRAMS

senior citizen centers
parents or staff at child care
    centers
cultural programs
community service
    organizations
soup kitchens
homeless shelters
food pantries

Arranging the Interviews

When I communicate with families and colleagues about interview possibilities, I'm not one teacher working alone but have perhaps fifty or sixty adults searching for people to interview and for other resources. Here are some strategies for getting help arranging interviews.

Learning About the Families

At the beginning of each school year, I send home a family survey. I design it to get the particular information I want. The year we studied about the histories and cultures of our families, the survey was about family backgrounds. If the study is about jobs, the survey will ask families about their jobs. Usually I add a second part to the survey asking for classroom volunteers.

From these surveys I get an idea of the resources available within the families of my students. For planning purposes, I make an informal chart about our class families. I jot down information such as who is willing to be interviewed, how each family volunteered to help in and outside of our classroom, and times people are available. For our People at Work study, my chart lists the types of work done by various family members. For a cultural or immigration study my chart includes information such as countries of origin.

Just a word of advice. Families come in different shapes and sizes. There are a growing number of divorces, stepparents, and other arrangements. Be sensitive to this when you write your survey so that people won't feel offended and everyone will feel welcome. For various reasons, a mother may leave the section about the father blank. That's okay. In my class, it's just a survey for my use. You have probably noticed that in this book I usually use the word *family* rather than *parents*. This comes from years of working with children who are not living with their birth mother or father.

Families as Co-workers

At the beginning of the school year, I make it clear to the families that I view them as my co-workers. I tell them that by putting their resources and life experiences together with mine, we can give more to their children. Families are welcome in our classroom. In fact, on the first day they can walk right into our room with us for a welcome meeting.

Social Studies Survey
During the year we will be doing research about our families.
You, the families, are an important source of information about
so many things. We value your participation in our social studies
thematic studies.

(*Please feel free to fill out only the parts of this survey you want.*)

Name of child _____

Country or place of origin of mother or guardian _____

_____

Country or place of origin of mother's or guardian's mother

_____

Country or place of origin of mother's or guardian's father

_____

Country or place of origin of father or guardian

_____

Country or place of origin of father's or guardian's mother

_____

Country or place of origin of father's or guardian's father

_____

Would any members of your family like to be interviewed by our

class in school or at your place of work? _____

_____

Survey about family backgrounds.

Communicating Regularly with Families
Establishing a good rapport with families is crucial. Early in the morning and after school I linger in the schoolyard or classroom so that I can talk with the families. Or I write notes to or call families whose children are bused to school. In addition to talking about their children, we discuss the ongoing research. I ask them to come for interviews. Often, I ask family members if they will help us arrange interviews with people they know from outside the school.

Family Homework
As a parent of three sons, I was constantly frustrated by the rather limited responses to my question, "What did you do in school today?" Often the answer was, "Nothing." *Family Homework* is my answer to this problem faced by so many families.

   Family Homework is the vehicle I have developed to enhance communication. On their first day in my class the children receive a copy of *Family Homework*, a weekly bulletin about our class. The first issue of *Family Homework* informs the families of our inquiry-based theme for the year and invites them to participate.

   The weekly *Family Homework* is a way of reaching all the families consistently. Subsequent issues of *Family Homework* provide updates about interviews held the previous week, some of the content of the interviews, issues to talk about with their child.

   In first two or three pages of *Family Homework*, I tell the families what we have done in each curriculum area and what we plan to do the next week. I let families know about the work of our various research groups. I attach two or three pages of homework, most of which is directly related to our thematic study. On Mondays I send *Family Homework* home in folders. The homework assignments are due on Fridays. For those families who can't fit the homework into their work schedules, I ask them to do the homework with their child during the weekend and turn the homework in on Monday.

   It is not necessary for every teacher to have such a long and detailed *Family Homework*. An abridged version would be very useful, too.

   Family Homework enables families to connect with their child's daily learning experiences. Families who are kept informed about the ongoing work in the classroom have a good way to launch a conversation with their child. An informed parent can ask specific questions such as, "Tell me about Elisa's job doing radio advertising" or "I wonder what it's like having two jobs like Alina's father, Ken." In addition, families who are kept informed are more likely to participate in some way.

Through *Family Homework* I can communicate with families about ways they can participate: sending in resources, coming to be interviewed, planning or attending trips, attending special events, and so on. Families are invited to attend upcoming interviews or to help in the classroom at any time. They are urged to help us find additional people to interview.

There is a formal thank you in *Family Homework* for anyone who is interviewed or who helps in any way. Many parents have told me how much they and their children love to see their names there and how much they appreciate the thanks.

Families react differently to *Family Homework*. Some have told me they can't wait for Monday to see the new issue. Others—only a few—are too busy or are not interested.

Communicating with Colleagues

My colleagues usually know what my class is studying. At Manhattan New School, we share this information at faculty conferences. Of course, there are the early morning, lunchtime, and afterschool discussions with colleagues in classrooms and hallways, too. Over the years colleagues have been very willing to share resources and suggest people for interviews.

Getting the Word Out

At Manhattan New School teachers post signs near the main office listing their classes' topics of study and asking for resources. This is a tremendous help, expanding the outreach from a single class to twenty classes and their families.

Setting up a School Database

Our school has a huge bulletin board listing all the languages other than English that are spoken by the families of Manhattan New School. Under each language are listed the names and countries of origin of the students. This was particularly useful to me when my class was doing a cultural study. Also, I was able to get the help of families for translation during interviews.

Our principal, Shelley Harwayne, serves as a human database. She interviews families when they enter our school. So if we are looking for someone to interview about a particular job or a particular culture, Shelley can often tell us the name of an appropriate family from another class.

Any school can set up a bulletin board or a computer database that would help classes find resources for their various topics of study.

Whom Did We Interview?

African and African-American Study

This was a three-month chunk of our year-long study We're All One Family Under the Sky. I hadn't intended it to last so long, but the level of interest of the children, the families, and myself was extremely high. Over the course of this three-month study our interviews included the following:

INTERVIEWS WITH FAMILY MEMBERS

Pia, Elizabeth's mother, is African-American. She grew up in New York City.

Michael, Angela's father, is African-American. He grew up in New Orleans.

Karen, Rashad's mother, is African-American. She grew up in Brooklyn.

Joan, Jhordan's mother, had been to several African countries. She is from St. Lucia and grew up in the United States.

Derreck, Jhordan's father, is African-American. His family is from Bermuda and North Carolina. He grew up in the United States.

Antoinette, Derrel's mother, is African-American. Her family was part of the Great Migration from the South.

Larry, Rashad's uncle, is African-American and grew up in Brooklyn. He is a high school teacher. He has visited Senegal in Africa.

Virginia, Rashad's grandmother is African-American and is a teacher.

INTERVIEWS WITH SCHOOL STAFF

Ida, a security guard, is African-American and was involved in the sit-in at Woolworth's in Greensboro, North Carolina, in 1960.

Constance, an English as a Second Language teacher, served in the Peace Corps in Cameroon in Africa.

Vickie, a paraprofessional, is African-American. Her family had a farm in North Carolina and now lives in Connecticut.

INTERVIEWS ARRANGED BY FAMILY MEMBERS

Sandra, a former co-worker of Jhordan's mother, was born and raised in Mauritius, off the coast of Africa. This interview was arranged by Jhordan's mother.

Philip, a friend of Derrel's mother, is from Haiti and is currently a day care teacher. This interview was arranged by Derrel's mother.

Members of the staff at the Apollo Theater in Harlem, interviewed at their place of work. These interviews were arranged by Jhordan's mother.

Caribbean, Central America, and South America Study

This was one chunk of our year-long study We're All One Family Under the Sky. Interviews during this study included the following:

INTERVIEWS WITH FAMILY MEMBERS

Four parents, from Puerto Rico, the Dominican Republic, and Peru).

A grandmother, from Puerto Rico.

Paola, Virgilio's cousin, who was on vacation from school in the Dominican Republic.

INTERVIEWS ARRANGED BY FAMILY MEMBERS

Eva, Alex's babysitter from Dominica. This interview was arranged by Alex's parents.

Tricia, Alex's new babysitter from Trinidad. This interview was arranged by Alex's parents.

Yvette, Stephanie's babysitter from Trinidad. This interview was arranged by Stephanie's parents.

Carlos, a doorman in Haden's building, from Puerto Rico. This interview was arranged by Haden's mother.

Ricardo and Katherine, neighbors of Charlotte's. Ricardo is a musician from Puerto Rico. Katherine is a dancer and educator. We interviewed Ricardo and Katherine and then danced, sang, and played Ricardo's instruments. This interview was arranged by Charlotte's mother.

OTHER INTERVIEWS ARRANGED BY MYSELF

Natacha, a student teacher from Haiti.

Shopkeepers at a Caribbean Market, La Marqueta. Family members joined us and helped explain things at the market. They also served as translators.

In your community, you may not have such a diverse population. But remember that in selecting an inquiry-based theme, we need to take into account the people and resources around us. I developed this year-long theme because I knew that in New York City I would have access to a broad range of people.

Your family studies or jobs studies will be different from mine and will have a character of their own. There is no rule stating that classroom interviews must represent great diversity. However, when we seek diversity in our inquiry studies, we bring into our classroom new or different perspectives and expand our horizons.

Flexibility Is Important

Over the years my students have interviewed family members, babysitters, friends, school staff, public service workers, storekeepers, senior citizens, and neighborhood workers. They have come to our classroom. Flexibility is essential. We have been flexible about everything from time, location, length of interview, and bringing of siblings along to languages spoken.

Traveling to Interviews

When we really want an interview, we travel. We interviewed a grandparent in her fifth-floor walkup apartment because she had many things to show us from her country, Panama. We interviewed storekeepers at their work. We took a school bus more than six miles so that we could see all the things from the Dominican Republic in Katherine's apartment. We walked to Jan Hus Church to see a senior citizen program and a soup kitchen. We took a school bus to the Yorkville Common Pantry to donate cans of food and to interview people. We even interviewed workers in the middle of the Brooklyn Bridge.

Stephanie's father, Leon, who has multiple sclerosis, couldn't come to our fourth-floor room, so we squeezed into a small room on the first floor to interview him. Leon was a therapist and wrote articles for psychiatric journals. He used a scooter to get around and sometimes used public transportation. He told the children about the struggle to get public transportation made accessible to the handicapped, and we role-played his story.

Another time, we walked to the building where Alan's father was the superintendent. The basement apartment was filled with craft items and pictures of patriots and landscapes from his native Guatemala. Sonia, Alan's mother, served a snack when we arrived. Then all twenty-eight children found spots on the sofa and the floor, took out their interview journals, and interviewed Sonia about Guatemala.

Being Flexible About the Time for Interviews

Interviews usually take place first thing in the morning, when the children are especially alert. When a guest requests another time, I accommodate. Some parents have jobs with little flexibility, or they attend school. For example, Elizabeth's mother, Pia, took an early lunch hour, so we had a late morning interview with her. Stephanie's father arrived on his scooter for an eleven o'clock interview because this was the best time for him. Emily Arnold McCully, author of *The Bobbin Girl* (1996), came for a quick five-minute interview at two o'clock but ended up staying for half an hour when she saw how serious the children were about their study of child labor and sweatshops.

Inviting Younger Siblings to Come Along

Some parents work at home caring for their babies. We welcome the younger siblings to the interviews, too. Charlotte's mother, Alexandra, brought her young son, Julian. Haden's mother, Kempy, took time off from work and brought her daughter Colby. Alex's babysitter, Tricia, had to bring Alex's little brother, Mark, to her interview. We worked hard to keep him busy with building toys.

A Reward for Being Flexible: Our Construction Site Interviews

One year we were involved in our year-long cultural study. However, there was a construction site on 84th Street and First Avenue, near Manhattan New School, that would be a forty-three-story apartment

Lia's father, Anthony, and his youngest daughter, Julie, with Paula at an interview.

building. I couldn't pass up the opportunity for my students to observe. We visited the construction site at least once a week.

The children and I developed a special way of arranging interviews with the workers. We waved at the workers high up in the building. Nearly always, they waved back. Some workers saw us sitting across the street on the sidewalk drawing and writing our observations. They came by to say hello. I asked them if they would stop for a few minutes to answer our questions.

That's how the children met Angelo, the signal man for the crane tower, and Bob, the crane operator, who called down to us on the microphone from the fortieth floor, "Hello teacher, hello children. How're you doing?" We met Robert who had a dog in his huge cement truck, which had a heart painted on it saying Stephanie. We remembered that because we had a Stephanie in the class. We met Benny, a union representative, who dealt with matters of safety for the workers. We role-played his job right there in the street because it was difficult to understand.

The children's awareness about various cultures was high because of the current cultural study. They expressed concern because we hadn't met any African-American or Hispanic workers. The girls complained that they hadn't seen any women workers. I was pleased to see such concern by six- and seven-year-olds. I asked Angelo about this. He told us that there were two women at the site. He said there were people of different ethnic groups, but they were working on floors that were high up. Angelo suggested that we come by at noon one day, when the workers were going to lunch. We rearranged our lunch hour, and we stood at the entrance to the construction site. I stopped workers as they exited or entered. We met Joanne, who was working for the management. We met Jute, an African-American bricklayer. We met Danny, a Filipino cement inspector, and Alfredo, a cement worker from Puerto Rico. We met electricians, plumbers, and laborers—people of all different backgrounds. The children began to see that each worker had a very specific job.

One day the children were taking notes in their journals. Suddenly I noticed that they were asking the workers for their autographs. One worker asked, "Why me? Why would they want my autograph? I'm just a worker." I told him that was why they wanted his autograph. He was important for our city. I wanted the children to have respect for workers. He smiled as the children handed him their journals.

Developing a good rapport with the workers was essential. The children's behavior was important. The workers saw me draw the children over to them so that everyone was focused on the interview. They saw me call on the children in an orderly way to ask questions. The children had to be silent while others were asking questions or a worker was answering. They were not allowed to raise their hands to ask a question until the previous question had been answered. They were polite. On-the-street interviews are usually very noisy, so these rules helped the children stay focused. We always ended with a thank you. The workers appreciated this, and one interview led to another.

One day Shariyf was so enthusiastic about the construction site study that he asked Angelo if we could hold a signal man's hat. A few minutes later, our class had a brand new construction hat, which we used in our block area. Sammy later gave us another hat. Then the workers from the crane tower company mailed us a box of hats, one for each child.

We had our math lessons right there at the construction site. We counted the floors. We talked and wrote about the ordinal numbers as we looked at the first, second, third, fourth, and other floors. Back at school in the block area, children labeled the floors of their building.

Shariyf in the block area.

At Writing Workshop there were stories and poems about the construction site. As the building got higher, we could see it from our classroom window.

In the spring Zachary's father arranged with the management company for our posters and poems about the construction site to be installed on the wall of the construction site behind Plexiglass. By the end of the school year, the huge building was nearly completed. Bob and his crane tower were gone. The cement trucks were at another site. But the memories of this experience will remain with us.

Special Interviews

While most of our interviews are with class families, we have also had some "celebrity interviews," some of them arranged by students' families. The families were well informed about our research and the specific interests of the children through *Family Homework* and their children's talk at home. The word was out that we were looking for people to interview.

These interviews were special to me because they were with real people who were connected to something I had previously only read about. Such interviews might be special because the person has, in the public view, a kind of "star" status—a musician in a popular band or orchestra, a founder of an organization, a friend or relative of a scientist, inventor, athlete, musician, or dancer. Many families will know personally or indirectly some "stars," and they are usually willing to do the necessary leg work to arrange interviews with them.

Rachel Robinson

Our interview with Rachel Robinson, widow of Jackie Robinson, came about because of some class research. During an African-American chunk of We're All One Family Under the Sky, a group of children had done research about Jackie Robinson. Each day they shared what they had learned. On the anniversary of the day when Jackie Robinson broke baseball's color bar and became a major league player, there were articles in several newspapers about him. I noticed the name of his widow, Rachel Robinson, and the organization she had founded, the Jackie Robinson Foundation. Thus, there was a way to reach her.

The group of researchers wrote letters to Rachel Robinson, expressing their anger with the way Jackie Robinson had been treated. They wrote in invented spelling. I mailed the unedited letters with a cover letter, explaining that the letters were unedited because I wanted her to see the passion of my young students.

Soon we received a call from the Jackie Robinson Foundation. The caller said that Rachel Robinson had been touched by the children's letters and that she would try her best to come to our classroom for an interview. Weeks passed. I called and called. But she was a very busy person. Finally, at the end of June, when there were only five days left in the school year, we set a date for the interview. It would be three days before school ended, at 11:30 A.M.

Our group of researchers greeted Rachel Robinson with a bouquet of flowers as she entered Manhattan New School. She was a most beautiful and dignified woman, aged seventy-three. Families, the principal, other teachers, and students from my previous classes joined us. One of her first comments to us was, "Do you know why I came to your school? Hundreds of school children invite me to their schools each year. I don't have time to visit them because I am very busy. I decided to come to your school because of your letters."

Rachel Robinson (left), widow of Jackie Robinson, with Paula at an interview.

The children asked her how Jackie had felt when people threw things at him or cursed at him. Rachel told us that her husband did not fight back or talk back. Instead, he became even more determined to play baseball better than ever. They asked her about when he died, how he died, where he died, and how she felt when he died.

They asked how it had felt to be married to such a great man. She told them that it is not enough to be the wife of someone great but that you should also be someone special. She talked about her work as a nurse, as a teacher at Yale University, as a mother, and as a member of the Jackie Robinson Foundation. She emphasized the importance of education to both herself and Jackie Robinson. The Jackie Robinson Foundation provides college scholarships for many young people. After Rachel Robinson signed autographs for the children, we gave her two murals we had painted about her husband. It was an interview to be remembered.

Carlton Green

One winter we interviewed Carlton Green, a member of the Harlem Globe Trotters in the early years, when African-Americans were not allowed on the National Basketball Association teams. He lived in the building where Aaron's father was a building superintendent. Aaron's father knew from the *Family Homework* and from discussions with his son that we had a group of children doing research about African-American athletes.

Carlton Green told us about the discrimination the Globe Trotters faced when they traveled around the United States. They were turned away from hotels and restaurants because they were black. We role-played these stories. The NBA refused to allow black athletes on their teams. That was why the Harlem Globe Trotters was formed. Carlton Green told us that the NBA management used to schedule games for all-black teams at Madison Square Garden right before the all-white NBA teams played because the all-black teams were so popular with the fans and the management hoped the crowds would stay for the all-white games. But very often the crowds walked out. After that the NBA started hiring black players. This was a bit complicated for the children, but we role-played a simplified version of this story.

I had never known that the story of the Negro Leagues in baseball was repeated in other sports. Learning it at this interview was far more meaningful to me than reading it in a history book.

In *Family Homework* the week after the interview, the families were told about the contents of the interview, and I thanked Aaron's father for arranging the interview.

Dr. Winifred Latimer Norman

While walking down the street one day, Elliot told his mother, Peggy, about his research group, which was studying about Lewis Latimer, an African-American inventor who developed the carbon filament for the light bulb. Elliot's research group had already taught the class about Lewis Latimer. They had looked at filaments in several light bulbs. They had experimented with batteries, wires, and bulbs. They had painted murals about Lewis Latimer and Thomas Edison. A few children had written books about Lewis Latimer.

In *Family Homework*, Peggy had read that a group of children was doing research about African-American scientists. She remembered that Lewis Latimer's granddaughter went to her church, and she immediately called her and then called me at home. Peggy was bursting with excitement. I was, too. The granddaughter, Dr. Winifred Latimer Norman, was eighty-one years old, a retired social worker with an honorary degree in humane letters from the Meadville-Lombard Theological School. For many years she had worked to preserve the legacy of her grandfather. I called her to arrange the date and time for an interview.

The children had an opportunity to hear about her great-grandfather, George Latimer, who escaped several times from slavery. During this interview, we role-played this story, and the children eagerly took notes in their interview journals.

In *Family Homework* families were told about this interview and were asked to discuss it with their children, and I thanked Peggy for her help in arranging this interview.

Sharrell Mesh-Alexander

During another African-American study, I informed the families in *Family Homework* that a group was doing research about Alvin Ailey. Charlotte's mother, Alexandra, told me that a woman in her building was a former dancer with the Alvin Ailey Dance Company. Would we want to interview her?

Sharrell Mesh-Alexander had been a premier dancer with Alvin Ailey Dance Company for twelve years. At age five she had seen Alvin Ailey on TV and dreamed of becoming a dancer. I asked the children if this reminded them of anything. Leonela said, "The poem." She was thinking of "Dreams," by Langston Hughes. After I complimented Leonela for helping us make this connection, we recited the poem for Sharrell.

Then Sharrell told us about her audition to get into the Alvin Ailey Dance Company. There were three hundred dancers at the audition. She was one of six to be selected. We stopped to role-play an audition so that the children would understand the concept. The children asked Sharrell about her travels with the company. She had traveled around the world three times. The children recognized the names of the countries from their previous map work and interviews. We stopped to look at the map on the wall.

A month before this interview the children had done research at home about African-American musicians. We had thought together about ways we could learn about musicians: record jackets, CD covers, cassette covers, books, magazines, interviewing people, movies, videos, and listening to music. I had offered my resources, including books, tapes, and records. Children had presented their

Sharrell Mesh-Alexander, former premier ballerina with the Alvin Ailey Dance Company, teaching dance at the interview.

reports, and then we had enjoyed the music together. We heard the music of Natalie Cole, Stevie Wonder, Whitney Houston, Diana Ross, Paul Robeson, Billie Holiday, Ray Charles, Wynton Marsalis, Louis Armstrong, and others. During the interview with Sharrell the children asked if she knew those musicians. Yes, she knew Wynton Marsalis, Stevie Wonder, and Ray Charles personally. We put on records and tapes of these musicians, and Sharrell choreographed dances for us.

I described the interview in *Family Homework* the next week and publicly thanked Alexandra for arranging this interview. Sharrell brought her young son to our next family celebration. We presented her with a copy of our homemade book *Sharrell Was an Alvin Ailey Dancer.*

> Sharrell Was an Buyouteful Alvin
> Dancer. She Dance good BeCuaes When
> She jops and hre body goes hlyre
> and that is good for hre.
> When She Prentedid She
> Was rech Sun MaeCk hre
> it IS reyol.

> Sharrell was a beautiful Alvin Ailey
> dancer. She danced good because when
> she jumped, her body went high.
> When she pretended she was reaching the sun,
> she acted like it was real.
>
> Moises April 3

Moises' page from the homemade book *Sharrell Was an Alvin Ailey Dancer* (April).

Interviewing Colleagues

Reaching out to colleagues at one's own school is important. You never really know the people in your own school until you begin to ask questions. Some may prove to be very important resources.

Vickie Carter, a Paraprofessional

I asked Vickie Carter to come for an interview during the African-American chunk of our thematic study We're All One Family Under the Sky. Vickie was a paraprofessional in the special education class.

This interview was particularly interesting. Vickie's great-great-grandparents had been slaves. She knew that they had been forced to use their slave master's surname, Carter. Almedina said to Vickie during the interview, "That's how George Washington Carver got his last name." One of our research groups had read that George Washington Carver got his last name from his master, Moses Carver.

Vickie told us she used to visit her grandfather on his farm in North Carolina, where he grew collard greens, beans, watermelon,

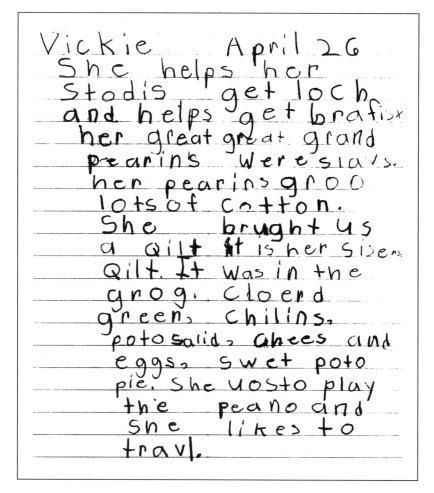

Vickie   April 26
She helps her
stodis get loch
and helps get brafist
her great great grand
pearins were slavs.
her pearins groo
lots of cotton.
She brught us
a qilt it is her sizens
qilt. it was in the
grog. cloend
green, chilins,
poto salid, ghees and
eggs, swet poto
pie. She uosto play
the peano and
she likes to
travl.

Alexandra's journal entry about Vickie Carter (April).

cantaloupe, cotton, and peanuts. Children from the George Washington Carver research group were amazed. They pointed to the huge mural they had painted just weeks before. The mural was in two layers, one with peanuts growing, the other with cotton growing. We had glued on real peanuts and cotton. By lifting the layers up and down to alternate them, one could see the concept of crop rotation, which George Washington Carver had developed to help struggling black farmers after slavery had ended.

Alex called out, "Just like George Washington Carver. Cotton and peanuts, cotton and peanuts. Cotton and peanuts." The whole class spontaneously joined in the refrain, "Cotton, peanuts, cotton, peanuts." I pointed out that George Washington Carver had, in a real way, helped people like Vickie Carter's grandfather and great-grandfather. This was a special moment. It was like a history book unfolding in our classroom.

Vickie told us that at her college in Vermont her dormitory was formerly the home of abolitionists. There were secret compartments for slaves to hide in. The house was maintained as a historic site so that the college students and others would have an opportunity to learn about the horrors of slavery and about the abolitionist movement.

Alex and Shariyf burst out, "That's like where Harriet Tubman hid!" The children from the Harriet Tubman research group told Vickie about their research. Again, the children saw the connection between their research and real people.

Ida Mae Chaplin, a Security Guard

One day Ida, the security guard at Manhattan New School, and I were chatting, as we did every morning. Ida said she was busy at her church making preparations for the Martin Luther King, Jr., celebration. As she talked, I knew I wanted to ask her to come in for an interview. We had already done a number of role plays about the civil rights movement. At the interview, Ida told us about her participation in the famous sit-in to integrate the lunch counter at Woolworth's in Greensboro, North Carolina, in 1960. We role-played the scene and "rearrested" Ida. Someone called out, "That's just like what happened to Rosa Parks!" Many of the children were getting good at finding connections.

Ida told us that Dr. King had met with the resisters the next week to encourage them to continue working to end segregation. The children were amazed to learn that Ida had been in jail and that she had met Dr. King. I later found Ida's picture in the book *Martin Luther King, Jr., A Documentary . . . Montgomery to Memphis* (Schulke 1976). There she was, her hair covered with the lemon meringue pie thrown at the demonstrators. The homemade book we wrote about Ida was called *Ida Is Our Hero*.

Celebrating the Learning

There is talk all around. It's time for a family celebration. Several notices appeared in *Family Homework*, followed by phone calls to class

*You are invited
to a Family Celebration
of our research about*

People At Work

Tuesday, May 20, 1997
5:30 - 7:30 pm
In the auditorium and room 407
Manhattan New School
Dora and Paula's class

* *Come see the new video of our play, <u>Let's Stick Together!</u>*
* *See the Channel 5 News video of our class trip to the
    Jackie Robinson Memorial Game at Shea Stadium!*
* *See our two original plays about Jackie Robinson and
    George Washington Carver.*
* *Sing.*
* *See our murals and other research projects.*
* *Enjoy a celebration feast.*
* *Be together.*

RSVP, room 407

Invitation to a family celebration.

families. Family celebrations are joyous events, taking place two or three times a year.

A family celebration is our ritual for highlighting what we have done so far in our inquiry study. For example, one November, we wanted families to see and to celebrate what we had done so far in our People at Work study. Another year we had family celebrations at the end of each chunk of our study We're All One Family Under the Sky.

At our family celebrations there are families, neighbors, babysitters, colleagues, and friends. I introduce the people we have interviewed. Families have read about them in *Family Homework* and in our homemade books. Now they can connect the reading with real faces.

The children sing songs and recite poems from our study. They may present homemade plays about their research. The hallway is filled with smells of the many foods contributed by the families. I thank families who have helped in any way—sending in resources, coming for interviews, arranging interviews, going on trips, or helping in class.

We present special honors. For example, we honored Ida Mae Chaplin for her participation in the Woolworth's sit-in in 1960. We honored Nat's mother, Alison Fraser, for helping us produce our play *Let's Stick Together*. For three years we honored Dora Cruz for working daily in our classroom.

The classroom is filled with our collective work. Research projects are on display—murals, big and small books, dioramas, homemade shoebox movies, posters, and crafts.

At the first family celebration they attend, families may not know each other. But by the second or third celebration of the year, they have already met in class and on trips, at schoolwide events, and in the schoolyard. Children have had play dates and sleepovers. There are bonds between families, and between families and myself—bonds that may last a lifetime.

A View from a Parent
Jhordan's mother, Joan, became involved right away in our thematic study We're All One Family Under the Sky. She had a flexible work schedule, so she was able to spend time in our classroom and help in the PTA. Joan was one of the parents who looked forward to reading *Family Homework* every Monday and seeing how she could get involved. Over the course of the school year she participated in many ways.

- Was interviewed about her country, St. Lucia, during our study of the Caribbean Islands, and about her job as an interior designer

- Arranged an interview with a former co-worker, Sandya, about her country, Mauritius, during our study on African history and culture

- Was interviewed about her trip to Africa, then cooked Senegalese chicken with the class

- Brought in paintings, carvings, and cloth from different countries in Africa and from Haiti

- Sent in records, books, and newspaper articles related to our topics of study

- Read to the class during Meeting Time

- Arranged and joined us on a trip to the historic Apollo Theater in Harlem

- Joined us on other class trips

- Encouraged other families to participate

In a letter to the Manhattan New School principal, Shelley Harwayne, Joan expressed her enthusiastic approval of her son's first-grade experience, including Family Celebration:

> I am writing . . . this letter because I feel it is crucially important to identify and show, as our experience in Paula's class did, what truly multicultural-based, quality education is. You see, one of the new understandings I learned is that a multicultural-based education is about starting from a premise that our city and world is made up of a multitude of cultures. That each cultural grouping or position can be a starting point from which the rigorous application of teaching and learning methods can take place and that through this specific application information and learning in the traditional disciplines of science, math and language, . . . takes place. It was also interesting for me to realize that out of that rigorous application of learning (which is . . . one of the reasons why we have our children at MNS) has come for us greater tolerance and appreciation for one another and lifelong learning.
>
> There is one additional aspect of the whole language/whole child teaching method on which I must

remark. That is the opportunity for expression, exploration, and development within each child for his writ-
ing/thinking/working intellect and voice. As I am
observing this phenomenon in the children and classes at
MNS it seems the most natural progression of learning for
the development of future adult minds. Yet, upon reflection on my [own] very typical schooling experience, it was
not until much later that students were asked to write from
within our own voices. It was much harder to do at this
later stage.

. . . While the first celebration was warm, in contrast, by
the evening of the final celebration we, the parents, were
thoroughly celebrating the new knowledge and skills our
children had learned. We were also celebrating the new
skills and growing we too had acquired. Even more impor-
tantly, the way we had grown in our awareness and appreciation of each other's individual background and cultural
nuances had transformed the parents in our class from a
tolerant, curious group into a lively, joyous, beaming, at-
one with each other group. It would have been impossible
not to notice how individual parent's eyes smiled and softened when their eyes met those of another parent—and
they smiled with their eyes at each other. Adult gazes also
softened as they looked at not only their children but each
of the other children in the room. For weeks after the celebration we talked among ourselves about the special feel-
ing of oneness that was in the classroom.

4 Strategies for Interviewing

Acknowledging Prior Knowledge

Just as each child brings prior knowledge and skills to a new inquiry study, so does she bring them to an interview. We are not starting with a blank slate.

The prior knowledge at an interview may have come from:

belonging to the family of the person to be interviewed

being a friend or acquaintance of the person to be interviewed

having a family member with the same type of job, hobby, or talent

having a family member or friend with a similar disability

having a similar ethnic or national background

speaking the same language

having lived in or visited the same country, city, town, or rural area

having experienced a similar adversity—living in a homeless shelter, being hungry

learning during previous interviews or research in school or at home watching educational television or movies

reading books and newspapers at home or in school

visiting museums, galleries, zoos

working with maps

being skilled at linking information or finding commonalities

As I have improved my skills for conducting interviews, I have come to see how important it is to value the children's prior knowledge. It gives me a better idea of how to proceed. To the children, it feels good to have prior knowledge. In fact, when the children know that I will ask about their prior knowledge, they think more actively. Children are then empowered to teach each other and their teacher.

Before we asked Rachel Robinson even one question at her interview, I asked, "Boys and girls, you have done a lot of research about Jackie Robinson. Before we start the interview, let's tell Rachel Robinson what we already know about her husband." Not only did it fill her heart with joy that the children were so well informed and so conscious of the issues of prejudice and segregation, but also this informed her where to start with us. She knew that she did not have to start from the beginning. She knew that we didn't have to define terms. The fact that the children had so much prior knowledge made it possible for us to go into greater depth at the interview.

At an interview with Lauren's father, Greg, about his family background, I said to the children, "Lauren's grandfather lived in Scotland. Here is Scotland on the map. Before we interview Lauren's father, let's tell Greg what you already know about Scotland." One child looked at the map and said, "Scotland is on an island." Another said, "There must be a lot of fish 'cause there's so much water." Greg would tell us later about the huge fishing industry in Scotland.

A child said, "There must be lots of beaches. Look at all of the ocean." Invariably someone said, "There are flowers in Scotland." I asked, "How do you know there are flowers? You can't see that on the map." The answer: "Well, people in every country love flowers. So there are flowers, even if people have to import them."

Children said there is music and dancing in Scotland, because they knew from previous interviews that people all over the world love singing and dancing. Children link the information. They see commonalities in the human experience.

I complimented the children for sharing their information with us. I told them that they already knew a lot about Scotland even though we had never talked about Scotland before in our class. During the interview Greg told us more about these and other topics.

When we interviewed parents during our People at Work study, I wanted the children to think about the adults' parenting role as well as their formal jobs. Before we asked Jonathan's mother, Gloria, any questions, I asked the children, "What jobs do you think Jonathan's mother, Gloria, does as a parent?" Their list was long: clean the house, help Jonathan with his homework, wash the dishes, go shopping, pay the bills, read to Jonathan.

Then I said, "You kids know so much already. Now, who would like to ask Gloria what other jobs she does as a parent?" After filling us in on that, Gloria told us about her job as an assistant to an orthodontist.

In the next *Family Homework* the children had to interview one parent or adult and make a list of the jobs they do in the house. A number of mothers commented to me that they really appreciated this assignment so that their children could see all the work they do for them.

At subsequent interviews we didn't spend as much time discussing the person's parenting jobs unless there were some special issues. There was prior knowledge now, so we could touch on the parenting job briefly and go on to other things.

The day after Thanksgiving vacation each year is Manhattan New School's Grandparents Day. Cameron's grandmother, Mary, was visiting from Connecticut. She said she didn't want us to bother interviewing her because "I don't have a job." I asked her how many children she had raised. She answered, "Five." I asked the class, "Mary raised five children. Did she have a job?" The children were bursting to tell Mary about all of the jobs she did as a parent. We decided that Mary had a huge job. I knew Mary was smiling inside.

Helping Guests Feel at Ease

Our guest always gets the seat of honor, the big rocking chair at story circle. I sit on a chair next to the guest. The children gather on the carpet, interview journals in hand. If a child is related to the person, that child can sit right near the person on the carpet or on a chair.

For some people, the thought of being interviewed by children is scary. If someone seems particularly worried, I take them aside and assure them it won't be difficult. I might say, "We're just going to ask questions about your job" or "We're just going to ask questions about where you come from. Don't worry. You'll have a good time."

We greet our guest with a polite "Good morning."

As children are taking notes, I talk quietly with the person we are interviewing to make the person feel comfortable. Sometimes the person shares information with me. Then I must decide quickly whether to present this information to the class. Sometimes the information is too personal or not relevant to our study, or it may not be age-appropriate. But sometimes the most significant issues of the interview come from these informal discussions.

Alejandra's father, Angel, agreed to come for an interview about his country, the Dominican Republic. He had notified his boss at the grocery store where he worked in Brooklyn that he would be late to work. I reassured him in Spanish not to be afraid, that I would translate for him if he needed, that the children were really nice and would not ask tough questions. But he was so scared that I literally had to take him by the arm and bring him into the school building.

Elizabeth asked Angel, "Did your mother ever sing you a lullaby?" I translated. Then he said, "Si." Elizabeth said, "Would you sing it for us?" This tall, shy man sang in Spanish a lullaby his mother had taught him. By the end of the interview, Angel and Alejandra were showing us how to dance to merengue music. He had such a good time at the interview that he came back the next week to cook a Dominican dish with the children.

Debby, Max's mother, didn't want to come for an interview because she "didn't know anything" about Trinidad, where she had lived for fifteen years. I suggested several times that in fact she did know about Trinidad, certainly enough to teach first graders. I told her some of the questions that would come up: What toys did you play with? What games did you play? What kinds of foods did you eat? What kinds of music do they have in Trinidad?

When Debby finally agreed to come for the interview, I saw that her hands were shaking. We started with questions about foods and animals in Trinidad. She seemed more relaxed. Then we found out that Debby's parents were not from Trinidad but had come from China. Some of Debby's family customs were Chinese. We looked at our map and traced the journey from China to Trinidad.

We also found out that Debby's mother had left the family in Trinidad to find work in the United States when Debby was twelve years old. Debby and her siblings went to school and then worked in their father's candy store. There was little time for playing, so she didn't know many games.

I could understand why Debby had been uncomfortable before

the interview. It's important that teachers listen carefully and be sensitive in the way we handle problematic issues. I chose to say little about the topic of Debby's mother leaving. Instead I emphasized how Debby had worked hard to help her family.

When the children asked about toys, Debby said most of her toys were homemade. She told us about the paper boats they made and sailed in the streets during a big rain. The children begged her to teach them how to make paper boats. Right after the interview, we gathered around Debby to make the boats. A few months later we learned that Debby would take Max to visit Trinidad for the first time.

Asking Questions at the Interview

Children's ability to ask effective questions at an interview develops with time and practice. At first, many children are not quite sure how to formulate questions or what questions to ask. By the end of the school year, they are pros.

Focusing the Questions

The types of questions asked at an interview will depend on the thematic study. If our theme is People at Work, I want the children to ask questions about the person's job, questions about facts and about feelings:

What kind of work do you do?

What do you do at your work?

How did you learn to do that job?

Why did you choose to do that job?

Do you like that job?

Why are you working at two jobs?

How did you feel when the customer was rude to you?

How did you feel when you couldn't get the new job just because you are a woman?

Tell us about your other job as a parent.

Then there will be follow-up questions about the details.

If the class is doing research about immigration, the questions might include:

Where is your family from?

Why did your family come to the United States?

When did your family come to the United States?

Did the family stop at Ellis Island?

How did it feel when you left your relatives and friends?

How did it feel when you first got to the United States? Were you lonely?

Did you know any English when you got here?

What was it like in school?

If a question is unrelated to the main focus of the thematic study, I may say, "Let's save that question for when we're finished asking Denise about her job" or "You can ask that question. Just save it for a little while until we're finished asking Jonathan about growing up in Liverpool."

Or, if we are asking construction workers about their jobs, for example, and a child asks how many sisters and brothers they have, I may let her ask that question. Then I ask the child to think of another question just about the person's job.

While it's important to be focused, there is no need to be rigid and to restrict all questions to the topic of study. At the beginning of the year, some children will be much better than others at focusing their questions.

Modeling the Questions

A major job for the teacher is helping children develop their interviewing skills. While I like the children to ask most of the questions, I model questions so they can learn inquiry skills such as these:

What are different ways to formulate questions?

Which kinds of questions are about details, and which are about bigger, more substantive issues?

How can we ask questions so that we can learn details?

How can we be more sensitive when we ask certain questions?

How can we focus on our inquiry theme?

For example, I might ask questions like these: "Michael, will you tell us about your job?" "Mary, who taught you to do those great Irish dances?" "Esma, how did you feel when there was a war in your country?"

Or I may suggest a question. This is very useful for children who have difficulty formulating or thinking of questions. "Who would like to ask Michael why he decided to teach college students and not first graders?" "Let's ask Mary about the country where she was born. Who would like to ask her?" "Perhaps someone would like to ask Mary about the kinds of foods she ate when she lived in Ireland." "Let's ask more questions about Eddie's job at the union."

Shifting the Direction of the Interview

Sometimes I want to shift the direction of an interview. For example, if we are doing research about the Dominican Republic and the children are asking questions like "Where do you work?" or "What street do you live on in New York City?" I will intervene. I might say, "After this question, let's focus on the time when Yobany lived in the Dominican Republic."

When we interviewed Jhordan's mother, Joan, about St. Lucia, I knew she was anxious to tell us about her work as an interior designer. So I said, "We'll ask a few more questions about St. Lucia, and then Joan wants to tell us about her job."

Enabling Full Participation

Certain children tend to dominate discussions in every class. They always raise their hands with a comment or a question. But it's important to involve all children in asking interview questions.

Some children are eager to ask questions. But when they are called on, they seem to go blank. Either they have not formulated the question well in their minds or they want to ask but do not know how to formulate the question. Perhaps they don't know how to ask it in English. Maybe they just forgot the question. I give them a second chance by saying, "I'll come back to you in a few minutes so that you can think about your question." If I know that a child is having difficulty formulating a question, I help him formulate one.

Rehearsing the Questions

Asking focused, probing questions is an art. At the beginning of the year, there are fewer and less sophisticated questions. As the year goes on, the questions become more focused and more substantive. Children need to practice asking questions.

Sometimes we rehearse the questions ahead of time. We might take time the day before or even right before an interview to think of questions we want to ask. I might say, "Tomorrow we're going to interview people who are working on the Brooklyn Bridge. What do you want to know about their jobs? Talk to the person next to you about the questions you want to ask" or "Dora's friend Bobby will be coming for an interview in a little while. Let's think about questions we want to ask Bobby about his work as a sanitation worker. Talk to the person next to you about the questions you want to ask."

I like these small-group discussions because they give every child an opportunity to think of questions and to rehearse saying them. One child may need to practice with her partner saying questions in English. Another child may be very slow at formulating a question. In the one-to-one discussion she is safe and has plenty of time.

After those small-group discussions, we have a class discussion in which we state our questions. Sometimes I ask for additional questions about that topic so that we can get more information.

If a particular question comes out sounding mean or insensitive, we talk about this and either drop it or find another way to ask it. It is important for the children to learn techniques for asking questions in a sensitive manner.

Perhaps a child's question is irrelevant to the study. We talk about why a particular question isn't really necessary at our interview.

Writing down interview questions in advance can be useful. This enables the students and the teacher to be sure at the interview that they have asked all their questions. A teacher can take time to look at the list of questions for assessment purposes, too. Occasionally a student teacher or I will jot down the questions. Older students may want to write their questions in their journals.

The Teacher Serves as an Interpreter

One of my roles during an interview is to act as an interpreter—sometimes to translate from a language other than English, sometimes to translate into what I call "first gradese," the language of my first graders. From experience we come to know what young children understand. We know ways to interpret or present concepts to young people. Usually, the person being interviewed does not.

Some people want the children to learn everything about them. Children can't and don't need to know everything. Some of the topics may not be relevant to the thematic study. Some topics may be over their heads.

It is essential to slow the interview down and to stop occasionally to interpret or to check for understanding. Before the interview I quietly advise the person we are interviewing that I will be stopping occasionally to make sure the children understand. Of course, this slows down the interview. There is less time to present information to the class. On the other hand, we can be sure that what is presented is understood.

Using Drama to Build Understanding

Role playing has proved the most useful means for me to help children process information and deepen their understanding of concepts presented at an interview. Nearly everyone wants to have a turn in a role play. Young children are often quite literal. They need to see, do, or touch in order to understand. They need to repeat and review.

Role playing is developmental. Since birth, we have practiced acting. Babies fuss and carry on just to get a new toy or a special treat. Children develop their acting abilities when they play "school" and "house." The "going to bed" ritual brings out the best in acting talent. So, for role playing at an interview, we just need to set up the scene and begin. The children will do better with time and practice.

When I want to place emphasis on or develop a better understanding of a concept at an interview, we stop for a role play. I have to think quickly to set up a scene. I have gotten better at that over time.

Then I select the actors and actresses. I ask the children not to raise their hands for different parts. I make the selection. I whisper to the children what I want them to do and say. In the beginning, I may have to "feed" the words. As children gain experience role playing, I give them directions quietly, and the children do the rest, with great enthusiasm.

Here are some suggestions for role playing:

- Try to be inclusive when selecting actors for a role. During the course of the interview, try to involve every child in at least one role, whether he plays an individual or is part of a crowd.

- If you find ways to involve children who are reluctant or shy, you will win them over. So, instead of having only one child do a part in a role play, you might have three or four do it together. Being part of that group will be more comfortable for a reluctant child. She may have so much fun doing the role play that she will want to do another.

- Certain children always want to be "the bad guy"—the mean boss, the prejudiced person, the cop arresting the demonstrators. I like those children to take a turn doing more positive roles.

- Remind the children that they are just acting. While the story may be real, we are just pretending.

- If you want to do a role play during an interview and can't think of how to develop a scene, you may want to ask the person you are interviewing for a suggestion, ask the class, or skip it and come back to it another day when you have had a chance to think about it.

Role play about disabilities.　During our People at Work study, we interviewed Diane, a teacher at the Lexington School for the Deaf. She was explaining about the school's job placement office. She told us that a job coach is assigned to work with a person who is hearing-impaired. This person helps deal with employers—setting up interviews, helping at on-the-job training, and helping to resolve problems. I thought this was important for the children to understand, and I was sure that it didn't mean very much to most of them when Diane first said it. Also, I wanted Diane to address the issue of bias and fear of hearing-impaired people.

I told Diane we would stop to do a role play. For the first scene, Diane was the job coach and I was the employer. Diane is not a job coach at her school, but I knew she would know what to say. One of the children was the deaf person. Diane did most of the talking, made arrangements for the deaf person to get the job, and stayed with him during training.

The second scene was rather dramatic. I provide details here to show how I orchestrated the scene. Diane was the job coach, I was the biased owner of a pet shop, and Suzannah was the deaf person.

I tell the class, "Suzannah is deaf, not really, but just in this role play. She adores animals and wants the job at the pet shop that was advertised in the newspaper."

Suzannah giggles and says, "I really do love animals."

I continue, "Yes, Suzannah loves animals and knows a lot about them. I know she has hamsters at home. Diane is her job coach from the Lexington School for the Deaf. I am the boss at the pet shop. I don't really like deaf people, and I don't want a deaf person working at my pet shop. Remember, this is just pretend. Diane is going to try to help Suzannah get this job."

I whisper to Diane, "Call me at the pet shop and try to help Suzannah get the job." Diane calls. "Hello, I work for the Lexington School for the Deaf. I saw your ad in the newspaper for a job at your pet shop. I think I have just the right person for you."

"I do not want anyone who is deaf," I say. "I know they can't do this job."

"But Suzannah is so good with animals," says Diane. "She has pets at home. She knows a lot about animals."

I snap back in a nasty tone of voice, "I don't want her to work at my pet shop."

Diane continues, "Suzannah is hearing-impaired, but she is excellent at communicating with people. I'd really like you to meet her."

I tell the class, "Suzannah goes with Diane to the pet shop. The boss asks Suzannah to help the customers." I whisper to Suzannah to do whatever she has to do to communicate with the customers. She does. She uses lots of body language and gestures. I knew she would be perfect for this role, because she is very expressive and good with people.

Because I want to broaden the participation, I assign several children to be "the customers" who have come to buy a hamster. I tell them to look around at the pet shop, and after Suzannah's persuasion, I whisper to them to buy the hamster.

We watch the role play.

Then I say, "Wow, Suzannah did a great job. She's really good with the customers. I want to hire her."

I turn to the class and say, "Talk to the child next to you about what just happened in the role play."

I listen in on their conversations. Then we have a whole-class discussion. It is clear from the comments that the children could see the special importance of the job coach in breaking down the boss' fear and bias. The role play also helped the children see that a deaf person is a real person with communication skills, knowledge, and feelings. They were glad that the boss had hired Suzannah.

Role play about prejudice. When we interviewed Rachel Robinson, she told us that Jackie did not fight back or talk back when people hit him, threw things at him, or cursed at him because he was black. She said that he was determined to play baseball even better. This was an important concept for young children to understand. I stopped the interview.

I called on Chris to come up to the front to be Jackie Robinson. I told him to hold our wooden bat and pretend to be at home plate. He got in position to bat. I assigned a pitcher to throw a pretend ball. I told most of the class to be the angry crowd. I told them certain words to shout at Chris. I limited the types of angry words they could say, because I would not let them use derogatory words. They shouted at him, "We don't want black baseball players. Go away. Get out of here."

I asked Chris to do what Rachel Robinson said that her husband did, to swing the bat even better, to play baseball the very best he could. Chris did that.

I shouted to the class, "Look, Jackie Robinson hit a home run. Look at that." I cheered for Jackie. I motioned to the children to shout and cheer.

I continued, "Turn to the person next to you and discuss this role play." After that we had a whole-class discussion. Then I said, "Write about this in your journal."

Finding the "Teachable Moments"

Interviews are filled with special moments—moments when a person has said something profound or of great social significance. We must be on the lookout for these "teachable moments," for they are the essence of education.

A person may say something during the interview that doesn't sound special or extraordinary to the children, but the teacher may see great potential in the comment. It's like mining for gold. We need to extract that comment and process it with our students. This may mean doing a role play or taking time to discuss it. A brief comment by someone can become a building block for moral values about kindness, sharing, or doing for others. I believe it is these special moments, usually coming from ordinary events in our lives, that shape us and make us who we are.

Here are a few examples from my classroom.

Interview with Shane's mother, Susan. We were doing a cultural study. Shane's mother, Susan, had a very complex family history, with her people coming from here and there all over Europe. It was too complicated for my first graders, so we glossed over it. I wondered to myself what could possibly come from this interview. I suggested that the children ask about when Susan was a child in Indiana. Susan told us about how her family's house burned down and the neighbors pitched in and helped rebuild the house. There was a "teachable moment." I knew the children understood what Susan had said, but it had no special meaning to them. I thought it was important that we role-play this story: people working together and helping each other during a disaster.

Interview with Kate's grandmother, Dr. Barut. Kate's grandmother came for her interview loaded down with small picture postcards of

June 24
Rachel Robinson

Rachel Robinson
filt bad wen they
sid kerses to him.
And Jokie Robinson
did Rachel Robinson
filt so Bad
and Jakie Robinson
did hwen he had
a hart atak.
And hwen they
sid cersis

to Jakie Robinson
wel jakie dirind hit
the peeple he sid
to him silf
that he wil be
the gratist plдyer
in bosball.
and he was the
best pleyer in
basball. And hwen
Jakie Robinson
went il hem

Lee's journal entry about Rachel Robinson (June).

Turkey. I thought to myself, "Oh, no, what can I do? The children will certainly get bored looking at these many pictures of tourist sites." I asked her quietly to let the children ask questions before we looked at the pictures. What a powerful interview it turned out to be! Dr. Barut was brought up in Turkey at a time when girls were not allowed to attend school. We role-played this. Some of my students were shocked and outraged, as first graders can be. Dr. Barut told us that her mother had wanted to become a doctor but wasnot allowed to. She told how people worked with Ataturk to make Turkey more democratic. When a new govern-

kid folowd him.
And Jakie Robinson
Jot in alat news
papers. and Jakie
Robinson and Rachel
Robinson met in Kales
and then Jakie
Robinson and Rachel
Robinson wen they
were Jeronups
they Jot
mareed.

And Jakie Robinson
was born in 1919.
And Rachel Robinson
stilr member
Jakie Robinson.

Lee's journal entry about Rachel Robinson (June) *continued.*

ment was formed, girls were allowed to attend school. Then Dr. Barut became a doctor. That was a big concept. We had to stop, role-play, discuss, and discuss again. We never did get to look at the tourist postcards, but the children did have a lot to write about in their journals.

Interview with Byron's father. Byron, Sr., came for his interview with a very full and rich life to share. He had participated actively in the civil rights movement, leafleting in Harlem for Malcolm X and later

85

for Martin Luther King, Jr. How would I handle this? As the initial questions went along, I was looking for a "hook." Then Byron told us about his teacher at a local college, who advised him that he shouldn't try to become a writer but should just become a plumber. The children asked him why. He said it was because he was black. I knew this was a "teachable moment." Perhaps this was more important for my students to understand than the myriad of details about his very interesting life.

I stopped the interview. We repeated Byron's story and then took time right there during the interview to role-play it. I asked, "How do you feel about this, boys and girls?" They said they were angry with the teacher. Some felt hurt. I asked Byron what he had done about this. He said he transferred to another school, where he was encouraged to write and where he was treated with respect.

I asked the class, "Did Byron give up?" "No," they said. One child said, "You know, that was just like with Ataturk. Remember what Kate's grandmother said? He did not give up."

This was a great moment in my teaching, when children could see the connections in history.

Byron went on to tell us briefly about some of his civil rights work. I emphasized that he went on after college to try to make this world better for other people.

Interview with Amanda's father, Hugh. Conducting interviews is not always easy. Amanda's father, a Cherokee Indian, came for his interview with an attaché case filled with documents. Hugh seemed prepared to teach a college course about the American Indian Movement to these first graders. What would I do? I explained to Hugh that I would stop the interview to make sure they understood his answers and that we would do some role plays.

Out of the many details, I chose to do a role play about the Trail of Tears—the forced migration of the Cherokee Indians from North Carolina to many regions of the United States. Ours was, of course, a much simplified version of this tragic story. The discussions after that role play were amazing. Hugh told us that during that forced migration some of the Cherokees settled near where Manhattan New School is now located. In fact, a local park several blocks from the school is named Cherokee Park, to remind people of that history. That was fascinating to me. We would visit the park a few weeks later.

After the interview, Hugh and I were joking around. I asked him how much of what he had planned to tell us he actually did tell us. He said, "About one-nineteenth!"

Interview with Laura's father, Larry. At his interview, Larry talked at length about the details of his work as a lawyer. It was all very interesting to me, but I knew it was way over the children's heads. I listened carefully for one piece of information that would be particularly relevant to my class. I stopped Larry when he mentioned a specific trial where he had successfully defended some workers who had been fired by a major corporation because of their age. Age discrimination was one of the issues I had hoped to raise during our People at Work study. We role-played this socially significant case. I chose to skip the rest.

Interview with Jeffrey's mother, Gladys. Jeffrey's mother, Gladys, talked about her job as a housekeeper at the Palace Hotel in New York. She talked about how important it is to be decent to all the hotel guests, whether they are neat or messy, whether they are friendly or mean. We role-played this concept. During the discussion, Gladys said, "You've got to have heart for this job. You always have to try to do a good job." The children were ready for the next question, but I thought this statement was so important that we should take time to discuss it.

Working with Second Language Learners

One can find ways to communicate effectively with second language learners at interviews, whether they are children who don't understand English or interview subjects who don't speak English. These are some of the strategies I use:

Repeat what the person said.

Restate.

Do a role play and have a discussion afterwards.

Draw a picture on the board.

Use your second language skills for translation.

Invite another parent or an older child in the school to translate.

If only one child needs assistance, have the child sit right next to an adult who can translate.

When Virgilio's mother, Kilma, and his cousin Paola came for an interview, I was their interpreter from Spanish to English. My students

Virgilio, Kathy, and Katherine and Kathy's grandmother, Dora, helped. When Iliana's mother, Maya, who spoke only Bulgarian, came for the interview, we invited her son Sasha from the second-grade class to translate. Another time, Mehmet came from his sixth-grade class to translate from Turkish for his mother, Gul.

Finding Connections to Literature and Music

References to poetry, literature, and songs come up continually during interviews, so it wasn't a surprise when, during the interview with Jessica and Andrew's grandfather about his father's work as a coal miner, some children burst out singing our favorite mining song, "Sixteen Tons", by Merle Travis.

Whenever someone we interviewed mentioned a person who didn't like to work very hard, I would hear, "That reminds me of Anansi." We had read many Anansi tales from West Africa and Central America.

If someone we interviewed talked about a market, children would ask if we could recite the poem "Jamaican Market Bus," from *Not a Copper Penny in Me House* (1993), by Monica Gunning. If the person we interviewed had a cat, there would be a request for Marilyn Singer's poem "Cat" or other favorite cat poems. When Elizabeth's mother, Pia, told us that she played jump rope when she was a child, children were eager to recite Eloise Greenfield's poem "Rope Rhyme," from *Honey, I Love and other love poems* (1986).

When Jessica's father, Fred, told about his mother's work at the sweatshop in the garment district, children wanted to sing the song from our play "Let's Stick Together," which Nat's mother, Alison Fraser, had written about the book *The Bobbin Girl* (1996), by Emily Arnold McCully: "Bobbin in, bobbin out, all day long. We are mill workers, and this is our song."

Thomas, Max's father, told us that he was a child in Poland during World War II and that the war was terrible. The children asked to sing a song about peace, "Last Night I Had the Strangest Dream," by Ed McCurdy.

Alejandra's mother, Gabina, told us a story from her childhood that the children said sounded just like "Little Red Riding Hood." For a few days after that at Meeting Time, we read versions of "Little Red Riding Hood" from different countries.

In order to encourage children to find connections to music or literature, we need to create a literature-rich and music-rich environment. In my classroom we recite poetry, sing, and read or hear stories every day. When this is done consistently, the literature and songs pop up during interviews, in the hallways, on trips, and at other odd times and places.

There are several ways to help children make connections that I have found very useful:

- Model making connections. Many times I will say at an interview or at Reading and Research Workshop or at Writing Workshop, "That reminds me of . . . [a particular poem, song, or story]," and we might recite the poem or sing the song.

- Read new literature or sing new songs. Sheila's mother, Mary, brought a book, *The Sleeping Giant* (1991), to her interview. This folktale by Marie Louise Fitzpatrick takes place in Dingle Bay, in Ireland, where Mary lived most of her life. The story explains how the small island got its name, The Sleeping Giant. Mary read the story to us. After that we kept looking for stories about real places in the world.

- Compliment children when they find these connections. I might say to the child who thought of the connection, "Great thinking, Clive" or "Rosie, I love the way you thought of this poem." Children like compliments and are always on the lookout for more. Then the interest in making connections spreads through the class.

- Mention examples of making connections in *Family Homework* so that families can encourage their children to find connections.

How Long Should an Interview Last?

The interview with Byron, Sr., could have gone on for hours. However, it was my role as the teacher to limit the time, the quantity of topics, and the issues raised for first graders. The length of an interview will vary depending on several factors:

maturity of the children, their ability to concentrate
how much time the person being interviewed has available
class schedule
content of the interview
ability of the teacher to generate interest and understanding

At the beginning of the year, interviews are shorter. By midyear they usually last thirty to forty-five minutes. Some interviews with workers at the construction site were as short as five minutes because the workers had to get back to work. Then there were interviews where the interest level was so high we couldn't stop. The interview with Amanda's mother was so interesting to the children that they demanded we continue after they came back from Spanish class. This has happened on several occasions. We called them our "two-part interviews." These interviews were filled with activities, so the children were not sitting too long. Within those interviews there was role playing, singing, dancing, eating, playing of games, or even cooking. It's important to incorporate at least some of these more active forms of learning at every interview because they enable the children to process, to understand, and to retain the information. It also keeps them from getting restless.

During the interview I observe the class to be sure that all the children are involved and that the interest level is high. I actively move the interview along. When the children seem restless, it's time to say, "We will have one or two more questions before we finish the interview." As the children mature during the course of the year, they will be able to stay focused longer at interviews.

Taking Notes

Everyone can take notes. One of our jobs as a teacher is to help children see that they can take notes, no matter what their age or academic abilities.

Using a Journal

Years ago, when I first started doing classroom interviews, the children sat with clipboards and paper in hand. They put interview papers in a folder. What a mess. Interviews were not in order. Some were missing.

A spiral or bound notebook is much more practical. Ours is a lined steno pad, which we call the interview journal.

When we gather on the carpet for an interview, I write the name of the person we will interview and the date on the dry-mark board. The children copy this into their journals. We put the date of the interview so that we can look back and see the growth and development over time.

Stopping to Take Notes

Children record the information for the same reason any newspaper reporter takes notes—to be able to recall the information at a later time. For young people, stopping to record also gives them a chance to hear the information again and to process it. Generally, after I stop the interview for emphasis or understanding, I give children time to take notes. Often, I ask a child to summarize, or I summarize the information. Some children need to hear it a second time, some a third time.

Stopping the interview for note taking is crucial. Otherwise many children will simply listen and not record information. We must exercise judgment about what is and what is not important for the children to record. Some factors include

relevance to the focus of our research

possibilities for extending the topic or concept beyond the interview

social significance

age and maturity of the children

length of time we have been sitting at the interview

If you ask the children to take notes, and you see that many are not taking notes, it's usually because they do not understand the concept or they do not know how to formulate notes in pictures or words. You need to discuss the concept again or do a role play.

During our African-American family study one year the Manhattan New School cook, Azzalee Brantley, told us about her parents' farm in North Carolina in the 1940s and 1950s. She told us the names of the crops they grew. I stopped the interview so that we could go over the list of the crops: corn, collard greens, beans, peanuts, and cotton. Some children recorded the names of the crops very quickly. Others asked me to repeat the list more slowly. They needed time and repetition so they could process the information. At the beginning of the year most of the children would have drawn pictures of these crops. But this interview was in March, and every child used invented spelling.

After Azzalee told us about the animals on her farm, we stopped again. We reviewed the list of animals: pigs, cows, a mule, and chickens. The children recorded that information. I watched as they recorded. I said the names of the animals several times because I noticed that some children were recording very slowly.

After Azzalee told us that her father had been in the National Association for the Advancement of Colored People and used to drive other farmers to the polls to vote, we stopped to role-play and discuss this. Then I said, "Write in your journal about what Azzalee's father did so that people would be able to vote."

Especially at the beginning of the year, I prefer that the children listen first and then take notes when I stop the interview periodically. I have found that many new writers cannot do both well at the same time because they are preoccupied with figuring out which picture to draw or they are sounding out words. So, the first several months, I ask the children to put their pencils down when the interview subject is talking. There are a few children in every class who like to keep a running record of the interview. They rarely put their pencils down as they record nearly every detail.

Discussing Ways to Record Information

Note taking is developmental. Children walk into my first-grade class-room at different stages of literacy. Yet, at the first interview in September, all of them are taking notes. Pictures, letters, and words are all valid forms of note taking. Invented spelling is a great tool for young writers. Newspaper reporters, court recorders, and professional authors use some of the same tools as my first graders. Even artists take notes in the form of sketches. Rosie's mother arranged for us to interview a New York City street artist, Myron Heise, who pulled out a green steno journal in which he had sketched scenes and jotted down labels for paintings-to-be. These were his notes. No matter how we choose to record the information, as long as it's relatively accurate, it's fine.

Since each child has different writing skills, the teacher needs to provide strategies for everyone to record information. When we stop to take notes in September in my first-grade class, I ask the children how they think we can record the information. One child may suggest making a picture. Another child may suggest writing the initial consonant. Still another child may suggest writing the whole word. Each strategy is given praise. During Reading Time and Writing Workshop we work on strategies, and we develop a sight vocabulary and various phonics skills, many of which are applied when the children take notes.

Occasionally I write a word on the dry-mark board that I think is important for the children to see. Aside from these few words, I do not spell any others. I do assist children in sounding out words, but I have found that if I begin spelling words for the children, there will be no end to this practice.

Every time we stop to take notes at the beginning of the year, I ask that same question, "How can we record this in our journals?"

Later in the year, when most of the children are taking notes with words, I stop the interview and say, "Take time to record this in your interview journal."

It is important that the children develop a sense of independence. I want them to feel comfortable recording information any way they can. They need to know that they can record information without the help of a teacher. No one will be critical of their way of recording or their spelling. In fact, I don't send the interview journals home until June, to avoid the overly critical eyes of some family members who may insist on perfect spelling. However, family members are welcome to look at the journals in school.

After a short time, the children take pride in their notes whether they used pictures, letters, or words. As the year and the writing progress, there is a movement away from picture notes. Pictures are replaced by letters, then words, then sentences, then sometimes pages and pages of notes. When Derrel moved from picture notes to sounding out words in his interview journal, he said to me, "Look, Paula. I don't use pictures any more. Look at all of my words!"

Learning from Each Other's Notes

Sometimes, after children take notes, I read or have a few children read from their interview journals so that they can hear how their peers have recorded the information. We listen to the notes of children of a few different levels of skill. Children approach note taking in different ways. Some draw pictures. Some make lists of information. Others record in sentences. Some notes have many details, while others are quite general. Knowing that they may be called upon to read their notes to the class often stimulates better-quality recording.

The more sophisticated note takers serve as role models for the class. When children who are still taking notes using pictures see others taking notes with letters or words, they will usually try to do that, too. Often when children hear the more detailed notes, they will try to imitate that style of note taking.

After an interview many students like to show their notes to the person we have interviewed, and the person likes seeing the different ways the children have written about him.

Saying "Thank You"

I always make time at the end of an interview for the thank yous. Even thanking people is learned behavior. At interviews in September, the

Almedina's journal entries showing a progression from pictures to sentences.

thanks are simple. Later in the year, some are so profound they have been known to bring the person interviewed to tears (of joy).

Being thanked by the children means a lot to people. It makes them feel appreciated and important. It creates a bond between the children and the adults.

When it's nearing time to end the interview, I say there's time for one or two more questions. After those questions, I say, "Are there any comments for. . .?" After we interviewed Kate's grandmother, we heard comments like "Thank you so much for coming to the interview. You taught us so much" or "That was good that you got to be a

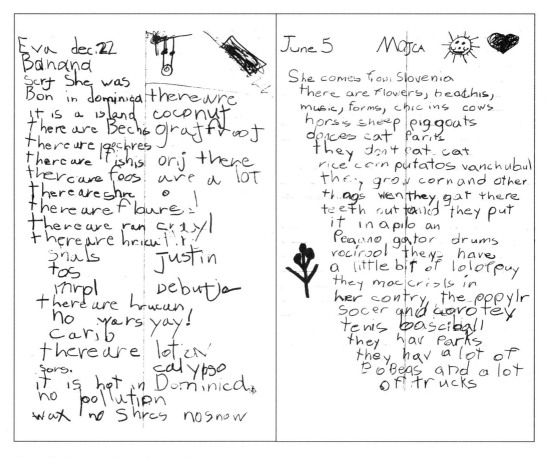

Eva dec.22
Bahana
Scrj She was
Bon in dominica there are
It is a island cocoonut
there are Beche grajfruot
there are poctnes
there are fishi orij there
there are foos are a lot
there are shre o
there are floures
there are ran crzyl
there are hriiul.r
snals   Justin
tos
mrpl   debutja
there are hrucun
no wars yay!
carib
there are lot cn
sors.   calypso
it is hot in Dominica
no pollution
wax no shres nosnow

June 5   Mojca
She comes from Slovenia
there are flowers, beachis,
music, forms, chicins cows
horsis sheep pig goats
donces cat parits
they dont eat cat
rice corn putatos vanchubul
they grow corn and other
things wen they gat there
teeth out tailed they put
it in a pilo an
Peaano gator drums
rocirool they have
a little bit of lolofpuy
they mac crisls in
her contry the pppylr
socer and gorofey
tenis bascibgll
they har parks
they hav a lot of
ßoßeas and a lot
of trucks

Almedina's journal entries *continued.*

doctor. Thank you for telling us about that." Then I asked all the children to say thank you.

Switching from questioning to commenting is difficult for some children. At first I have to interrupt a child who is asking another question. I may say, "I know you have another question, but we are not asking any more questions now. What would you like to tell ———— about the interview?" or "What would you like to say to ————?"

Dora Cruz is Kathy's grandmother and guardian. She was shy and didn't participate much in classroom activities. I wanted the children to

Kathy's grandmother, Dora Cruz, reads with Lee.

interview Dora. She was hesitant. By the middle of the interview, Dora was relaxed and was having a wonderful time. She smiled when the children thanked her. It meant a lot to her. The children ran up to her in the schoolyard. We talked more. One month later, I asked in *Family Homework* for volunteers to help us because we would have no student teacher for one month. Dora volunteered. She never left. Dora has worked full-time as a volunteer in our classroom for three years. She is a parent and a teacher to the children. She is my co-worker and friend. Next year, she will work full-time as a paid school-aide.

Planning the Day 5

Overview

With the hustle and bustle of home life, it's important to have a steady schedule, a predictable day, in school. During my first twenty years of teaching in New York City, I had little input in formulating my schedule. Nearly every period there was a pull-out program such as English as a Second Language or reading. Finding more than one period when my whole class was in the classroom was difficult. During those years, I had to eliminate unnecessary rituals, speed up transitions, and create small blocks of time for inquiry studies. This probably sounds familiar to many teachers.

At Manhattan New School we have a minimum of pull-out and push-in programs. My schedule has evolved over time. Even after four years there, I continue to experiment with the schedule. Sometimes the morning ends, the time has flown by, and we haven't done math. I sigh. That's frustrating. Sometimes I look up at the clock during Writing Workshop and find we have missed ten minutes of recess. It's difficult to maintain a workable schedule given a rigorous curriculum. However, I think that is a problem for most classes that become deeply engaged in their work. Your schedule has to work for you with your set of circumstances. We do the best we can.

The Schedule and Classroom Rituals

In this chapter I show our typical schedule and explain how I adjust it during the morning on interview days.

Before the children arrive, I write the date and our schedule for the day on a dry-mark board near the entrance of our room. Then I go to meet my first graders and their families or babysitters in the schoolyard. At 8:40 a.m. I blow a train whistle, the signal for the children to line up. As my class reaches the fourth-floor landing, we stop. I greet the children and briefly tell them how we will begin the day. I mention any special events. A calendar and a chart with the days of the week are near the entrance of our room. A few children take responsibility for writing the date on the calendar and for moving the huge clip on the day chart. The children will need this information throughout the day as they put the date in their journals and on their stories. Independently, they put their homework folders in the box, hang up their coats, and put the chairs back at the tables. Some children stop for a moment to chat, and then they set out to work.

Periods are approximately forty-five minutes. Fortunately, there are no bells at Manhattan New School, so that a period can be longer or shorter than forty-five minutes. There is some variation in this schedule because Specials are not at the same time each day. Since we formulate thematic studies around social studies topics, social studies takes place all day. In the next chapter I explain how we extend the content from the interviews into the various curriculum areas.

A typical day looks like this:

Period 1   Reading and Research Workshop (or interview)

Period 2   Handwriting Time or Science Workshop (book writing or cooking on an interview day)

Period 3   Math Workshop

Period 4   Specials (Spanish, art, music, gym, or science)

Snack

Period 5   Reading Time

Period 6   Writing Workshop

Lunch and Recess

Period 7   Meeting Time (poetry, singing, stories)

Period 8   Center Time

Reading and Research Workshop
We begin each day with Reading and Research Workshop. The children head for different bookshelves to gather books, magazines, at-

lases—materials for their research. Children get out their reading and research journals. During the workshop, children can read, do research, or listen to cassettes. They can work alone or with other children. They can sit at a table or on the floor.

The children know where to look for resources because we have practiced. During the first few months of school I introduce them to the Reading and Research Workshop. We talk about where to find different types of books or magazines, how to set up the tape recorder, how to record information, and where to return books. I keep my voice very low in order to establish a calm atmosphere in the room. Occasionally some children need a reminder about speaking in a quiet voice so that others can focus on their work.

Many times during Reading and Research Workshop, I stand back and look in amazement. The classroom reminds me of college. Some children glean information from pictures in magazines and atlases. Others work in small groups by themselves or with a parent or grandparent, a student teacher, or me. Some children read and reread poetry. Others gather to read and sing theme-related songs printed on charts around the room. Children at the listening center listen to music or stories. Usually there are one or more formal research groups, which always welcome new members.

Each child has a reading and research journal, an $8\frac{1}{2} \times 11$-inch spiral-bound notebook. As children do their reading or research, they record information in their journals. At the beginning of the year, most record with pictures. Later they record with letters, words, and then sentences.

During Reading and Research Workshop I work with one or two research groups, sometimes alternating between them. While children are recording information, I circulate around the room, stopping to hear a child read, asking a question, reading a journal entry, encouraging a reluctant worker, or giving compliments. When there are student teachers, they do the same. Often family members join us. Nearly half an hour flies by, and it's time to stop the workshop. I give notice that there are only a few minutes left. Then I give a special hand-clapping or voice signal that means stop work and put books, journals, and pencils down.

Each day Reading and Research Workshop ends with a ten- to fifteen-minute sharing time. It often begins with compliments. Sometimes I'll say they worked like college students—they love that. For sharing time, children remain where they have been working so that they are with their reading partner or research group and have their books and journals in front of them. I stand in a central location and

Derrel (left) and Clive share their research after Reading and Research Workshop.

give them an opportunity to briefly tell others what they have read, perhaps what they thought about a story, or why they had selected that one to read. Each research group has an opportunity to tell the class what it has learned and how it got the information. All attention must be focused on the person who is speaking. Since the children are scattered around the room, often I repeat what children say, emphasizing various points and checking to be sure other children understand.

During a study of the Caribbean Islands, Central America, and South America, children in one research group showed a map of the Dominican Republic that they had found in a *National Geographic* magazine. The map indicated where various crops were grown. We read the key together. We looked at pictures of these crops at the marketplace. When the group showed the picture of sugar cane to the class, some children were surprised to see sugar in its natural state and to find out that sugar is grown in Virgilio's home country.

Another group had learned more about Trinidad by rereading Lynn Joseph's poems and examining the pictures in *Coconut Kind of*

Day. Another group, which had worked with the student teacher, told us about some rain forest animals from Brazil. They had drawn and cut out pictures of each animal for their rain forest mural.

Often there is science, social studies, literature, reading, writing, math, or art right there in the sharing time. At the end of sharing time, children put their books and journals away.

Handwriting Time

Once or twice a week we settle down to develop the children's handwriting skills. Though it is not my favorite activity, the children love the compliments they get when they write "like a computer." Early in the year we work on letter formation and spacing between words. Later we work on the use of capital letters and punctuation. Often the words I select or the sentences the children copy, letter by letter, are related to our study. For example, if we are practicing when to use capital letters, we might copy the names of some of the countries or cities in our study or the names of people we have interviewed. We might write the title of a folktale we have read. We alternate between Handwriting Time and Science Workshop.

Science Workshop

Science inquiry time is flexible. Our science activities are based on the curriculum standards of the New York City Board of Education. Other science inquiry flows directly from the content of the thematic study. Sometimes we have a formal Science Workshop. Or children may read science books during Reading and Research Workshop or recite science poems at Meeting Time. Science observations take place during Writing Workshop or Center Time.

Math Workshop

Most days we have a formal Math Workshop, based on our district math program. However, math doesn't always fit neatly into Math Workshop. Math skills, math concepts, and critical thinking are an integral part of each thematic study and can come up at any time of day. Math comes up during interviews. There are math concepts in folktales, stories, and songs. Math comes up during trips. There are numbers, tables, and graphs in books and newspapers. Shapes and patterns are everywhere in the cultures or jobs we study: in the clothing, the art work, and the buildings. There are plenty of graphs to make and interpret. I am always on the lookout for natural connections to mathematics.

Each child has a math journal, a place to record math thinking. Children work in small groups or in pairs, recording as they work.

Specials

Every day the children go to a Special such as art, music, gym, Spanish, or science. I work closely with the teachers of the Specials. Whenever possible, they extend our classroom studies into their curriculum areas. The music teacher teaches the children songs from the region or about the topic we are studying. The science teacher often deals with science questions that came from our interviews or other research. In Spanish classes, the teacher tells her own family stories, reads folktales and other stories, and teaches the children the Spanish language through hands-on activities.

Snack

Because our lunchtime in some years is late in the day, at 12:35 p.m., the children need a small snack. Parents take turns bringing snack for the week. Crackers and fruit are the typical snack. However, some parents bring theme-related snacks such as tropical fruits or ices for our Caribbean Islands study. On the day of her interview, Virgilio's mother prepared rice and beans, salad, plantains, and chicken—Dominican style. During our European study, we ate Scottish and Irish breads. We smell new smells and taste new tastes. These ten minutes are a time for socializing, too—"breaking bread" together.

Reading Time

Reading Time allows for a more formal reading experience. Children read stories, poems, and songs. Two days each week we use the homemade books from the interviews for guided reading. (Chapter 6 provides more information about using homemade books.) The other days children read alone, with partners, or in small groups. Then they discuss the story and write in their reading and research journals. Groups and reading partners change depending on the children's needs. I work with struggling readers daily. Student teachers, school volunteers, family members, and reading recovery teachers work with groups or individuals.

Reading is a natural part of many learning experiences throughout the school day. There are reading activities during Reading and Research Workshop; during Meeting Time, when we read poetry or songs from charts; and during Math Workshop. In our whole language classroom, work on reading strategies flows naturally from the reading at hand, whether at our formal reading lesson or at other times during the day.

The selection of books is based on the needs, interests, and skill levels of the children. We use a variety of trade books and literature, only some of which are connected to our theme.

Writing Workshop

This is a favorite time for the children and for me. At the beginning of the year we have minilessons. Children gather at story circle for a quick, two- or three-minute introduction. In September minilessons are about management issues, such as where to get your writing folder, where to get paper, how to use the stapler, or places you can work. For example, the writing folders are color-coded. The orange dot on a child's folder means that the folder is in the plastic box with the orange dots. By the end of the first week of school, children can get their own writing folders, get additional paper if they need it, sit down at tables or on the floor, and get started with only a minimum of assistance from me. Pencils, crayons, and water-based markers are in containers at each table. I want the children to be in charge of themselves as much as possible. I always tell them to "be your own teacher."

With these management issues out of the way, the children have more time to write and I have more time to help children with their writing. Very soon minilessons include how to think of new topics, how to sound out words, or how to find words we need in our classroom environment. As children develop as writers, we get involved with editing and revision skills—the quality of the writing improves. Many times we skip minilessons and the children go directly to get their folders. This gives them more writing time.

Children select their own topics. Initially many of their stories are typical first-grade topics: their families, the park, friends, and pets. As our social studies research develops, other issues find their way into the children's writing. There are biographies and autobiographies, "how to" books, poetry, sports books, movie reviews, and writing in nearly every genre.

Invented spelling is a great tool for young writers. It enables them to express themselves with the skills at hand. Invented spelling frees the children to write without fear and to write about any topic or in any genre they wish. It frees me from the terrible burden of spelling words for them. Invented spelling puts the children in charge. It empowers them. Or as they often put it, "Paula, I can sound it out myself, it's not your job, you can go on vacation!" Student teachers, family members, and I circulate among the children, hearing them retell their stories, helping them with new skills, or just complimenting their work.

We close Writing Workshop with sharing time. Sometimes this is informal and quick, giving children more writing time. Children stay where they have been writing while I make a few comments about some of the highlights of the workshop. Perhaps I'll show Michelle's story in which she used her first exclamation mark, or hold up Alex's story to show how he worked hard to provide more detailed information in his biography of Jesse Owens. Perhaps we'll celebrate that a child has stayed with one topic for the first time. Often applause breaks out, and I can see a smile of newly born self-esteem in that author. After the informal sharing time, I remind the children to write their names and the date on their work, place it in their folders, and put their folders in the writing box. After a while, I remind them only about the name and date—the rest is automatic.

Some days we have half an hour of writing and a ten- to fifteen-minute formal sharing time at story circle. Children put their folders away and go to story circle. At story circle we share the work of three or four children. A child sits on our special "author's chair" and reads her story. The author then calls on two or three children for comments about the writing. This is a great time for building self-esteem. A child who finally started to focus on her writing becomes a hero. It is also a time to encourage the use of new skills. A child who just started using the quotation marks that we had discussed earlier becomes a great role model. A child who started to revise his writing sets a fine example.

As writing skills develop during Writing Workshop, I notice that journal entries at interviews and page entries for the homemade books become more sophisticated.

Meeting Time

Winding down from Lunch and Recess, the children hang up coats and go to story circle. I sit in the large rocking chair. The poetry shelf is right beside me. The children know just what poems they want to hear. We recite old poems and then I introduce new poems. I have printed many of the poems on a chart so that we can use them for shared reading. Many of the poems are related to our topic of study. We have several delightful books of poetry by poets of different races and nationalities. We make pretend raindrops fall for Langston Hughes' poem "April Rain Song," from *The Dream Keeper and Other Poems* (1994). Children dance to Shel Silverstein's poem "Rock 'n'

Roll Band" from *A Light in the Attic* (1981). They jump to Eloise Greenfield's poem "Rope Rhyme" from *Honey, I Love and other love poems* (1986). We make up our own summer verses for Marilyn Singer's "Cat," a winter poem, from *Turtle in July* (1989). The children love poetry. The first thing every day or at Meeting Time, children search for our principal, Shelley, to present her a gift of a poem.

Next, I take out my guitar. Each day we sing old songs, some of which are posted on charts. Then I introduce new songs, some of them related to our thematic study. Children snap fingers, clap hands, write adaptations, or act out the words of the songs.

Then, it's time for a story. As often as possible, stories are theme-related—an African folktale, a Native American legend, a European fairytale, a Caribbean story, stories of People at Work. Finding appropriate, well-written literature is important. Sometimes during the story I stop and ask the children to discuss something with the child next to them. After that we have a whole-class discussion. They might try to predict what is coming next in the story. They might try to figure out why a character does something. They might tell how they feel about what a character did. We end each story with small-group and then whole-class discussion about the book.

Center Time

This is a popular time of day. It happens around two o'clock, after a day of rigorous work. Center Time includes a selection of these activities:

painting at tables

mural painting

block building

dressup

listening center, with headphones, books, and tapes

science, including our pets, magnets, magnifying glasses, and books

crafts

writing or reading

computers

pattern blocks and other manipulatives

When Meeting Time is finished, I tell the children which of these activities are available that day for Center Time. There are six activities at most. When I restate the list, children may select that activity by raising their hands. That is a quick and easy way to do this, maximizing time to actually do these activities.

Often our thematic study flows naturally into Center Time. For example, children who choose dressup often retell stories we have read or role-play something from an interview. Children working with blocks might build ships exporting food, coal mines, or replicas of construction sites.

The murals we make at Center Time are nearly always theme-related. Chapter 6 provides greater detail about mural painting.

After a one-minute notice, I give a hand-clapping or voice signal. Center Time is over. Children who take the bus get ready to leave early. Children know that they are responsible for cleaning the area where they have worked or played, plus some of the common areas. They stack the chairs, pick up stray pencils or crayons, and straighten tables. Children know that they have to get their coats, take their *Family Homework* folders from the box, find a partner, and get in line. They are in charge. Of course, that is not automatic at first. We practiced it.

As children stand in line with partners, we sing an adaptation of a Woody Guthrie song, "So Long, It's Been Good to Know Yuh." We say good-bye for the day. Children are usually bursting with stories for their families and babysitters as we enter the schoolyard.

How Do Interviews Become Part of the Schedule?

The only major changes in our schedule are for trips or interviews. Keeping a steady schedule is important. Even an interview day has its own pattern.

Interview Days

Interviews usually take place first thing in the morning, replacing Reading and Research Workshop. At that time, the children are alert. Also, that early time enables the person we interview to hurry off to work or school.

After the first few interviews, children know just what to do to prepare for an interview in the classroom. Then when I stop as we come up from the schoolyard in the morning and say, "Today we will be interviewing Alina's mother, Yorlene. You don't even need a teacher to tell you what to do, do you?" They respond, "No. We don't need a teacher." They put their homework folders in a box, hang up their coats, put the stacked chairs back at the tables, get their interview

Alina and her mother, Yorlene, at an interview.

journals and a pencil, to sit at story circle, and copy the date and the name of the person we will interview. Our guest sits in the big rocking chair. I sit on a chair next to the guest. After a morning greeting, we are ready for the interview.

Writing About the Interview

After each interview we talk briefly about what we might write on our pages for the homemade book about the person we interviewed. Then the children sit at tables or on the floor to write their pages. Adults circulate among the children to help and encourage them. Children who finish early go to read independently. (Chapter 6 gives more information about writing homemade books.)

Cooking

Sometimes cooking is an extension of an interview. Jhordan's mother, Joan, stayed after her interview to help us cook Senegalese lemon chicken. Kilma and Paola stayed to cook plantains to go with the chicken, salad, and rice and beans, Dominican style, which they had prepared at home.

If during an interview the person tells us about food from his country, children invariably ask, "Will you cook that with us?" Michelle's mother, Josephine, returned a week after her interview to cook ftira with us, a kind of Maltese pizza. Alejandra's father, Angel, returned to cook a Dominican blue fish recipe. At several interviews, during a cultural study, parents told of memories of licking the cream off the top of the milk when they were children. I asked the families in *Family Homework* if any of them had similar memories and could get some nonhomogenized milk for us so we could have the same experience. Amanda's mother brought us some milk. This brought back memories for me, too, as I had enjoyed nonhomogenized milk as a child. We turned the remaining cream into butter.

Some thematic studies don't lend themselves to many cooking activities. During our People at Work study, we had very few theme-related cooking experiences.

While cooking may take time away from a formal Math Workshop, cooking is math. We measure. We count. We cut things in half and into other fractions. We handle two-dimensional and three-dimensional objects. Math is more fun than ever on those days.

Cooking is also writing and reading. We copy and read recipes. We learn the tastes and smells of foods from many cultures. We try new foods. I laugh when parents tell me their child would never try anything different at home. In school, it's "cool" to try something new. We learn to be polite when there are tastes we don't like—nasty faces and comments are not acceptable. We always share our cooking with the staff at school.

Keeping the Concepts Alive 6

Overview

During one school year my first-grade class did a study about People at Work. Of the seventy interviews we conducted, forty-five lasted one half hour or more. At each of these forty-five full interviews children took notes in their interview journals and then wrote pages for a homemade book about the person. In addition, there were several shorter interviews where no notes were taken. A wealth of information and many new concepts were gained from these interviews.

It's not necessary to have this many interviews. My problem was that once we got started, the children really pushed family members and friends to come for an interview. Many parents and other relatives wanted to participate. If finding people to interview is a problem, see Chapter 3 about ways to reach out to families, colleagues, and the community.

The content of each interview took on a life even after the person had left our room, because the content of the interviews became our curriculum. In this chapter I outline how this happened in the People at Work study.

What I have noticed over the years about this content-rich curriculum, this inquiry-based approach, is that it inspires the children, the families, and me. It makes learning and teaching exciting. In two previous schools where I taught, many teachers copied their lesson plans from year to year or simply followed along from curriculum guides. No wonder they felt burned-out after a while. I hope this book will inspire you to use an inquiry-based approach to education.

Self-esteem

Because the families play such an important role in the process, the children feel great pride. After her interview, Jeffrey's mother, Gladys, said that Jeffrey begged her to come for an interview because he wanted the other children to respect her work as a housekeeper at a major hotel. Gladys presented her job with such dignity that Sophie wrote on her page for the book about Gladys, "When I grow up, I want to be a housekeeper at a hotel, too."

Can you imagine being a young child, and your mother is sitting on the big rocking chair in front of all of your classmates? Then she is answering their questions. You act in a role play about your mother's job. At the end of the interview, someone tells your mother that she is going to be famous because the kids are going to write a book about her. Your mother will be the focus of reading lessons for two days. And the reading assignments in the next *Family Homework* are based on that book, so every family will hear their child read about your mother and talk about the concepts raised at her interview. Maybe the children decide to do even more research about your mother's kind of work. Or they might go to visit her at her job. Something your mother said may become a math lesson or a science investigation. Your friends may paint a mural about your mother's work. At Center Time children in the dressup area might be pretending to do your mother's job, and you join them in the fun. That can be a really memorable experience.

Teaching Academic Skills

When developing an inquiry-based curriculum, it is essential to be fully aware of the required skills and standards for reading, writing, math, science, and the other subject areas on the particular grade level. These lie at the heart of our curriculum. The contents of the social studies theme are the building blocks for that curriculum. And so, while we conduct interviews, while children work in small research groups, while I prepare our homemade books for publication, when I'm at the library or the bookstore, and when I should be fast asleep at night, I continually think of ways to extend the concepts from interviews and other research into every area of the curriculum. Our social studies–based study becomes an interdisciplinary curriculum.

Yes, I have a math program from our school district, and I implement this math program. In addition, some of our math activities flow from the interviews and other research. Yes, we use trade books and other literature for our whole language reading program, but we also use our homemade books. I'm always searching for literature, poetry, and songs that relate to the content of the inquiry study. Of course, it is okay to add stories, poems, and songs that are not related to the theme.

All of our inquiry work is interdisciplinary. An interview may involve social studies, drama, writing, reading, science, dance, cooking, or math. Making a page for a homemade book involves writing, reading, and art. The work of research groups may involve social studies, reading, writing, science, or art. Presenting research may involve projects using drama, writing, reading, or art. Painting a mural may involve social

The interdisciplinary nature of our People at Work study.

studies, art, science, writing, or reading. Social action projects may involve social studies, writing, art, math, science, or drama. I see our curriculum as an interconnected whole.

Making Choices

How do I decide what to do after an interview? That's not always easy. If each interview were extended fully into the curriculum, there would be an overabundance of activities. I must make choices. Some of the determining factors include

> relevance to the thematic study and overall curriculum goals
> the children's interests and skills
> the teacher's interests and skills
> other ongoing research projects and activities
> availability of people to help
> availability of resources
> time

Not every interview needs to be extended fully into the curriculum. Many interviews are not. When children take notes in their journals, we usually make a homemade book, which we use for guided reading. However, there may not be any further activities. This does not mean that these particular interviews were not significant. Every interview has significant issues and concepts. Each interview is a vital part of our research. While there may not be any specific curriculum activities, we may refer to issues or concepts from an interview over and over throughout the school year.

For example, the children already knew a lot about the job of building superintendent from their own experiences at home and from our December interview of Alina's father, Ken, who is the superintendent in five buildings. In January we interviewed Melisa's mother, Esma, who is the superintendent in three buildings. Alina's mother, Yorlene, works as a superintendent with her husband, Ken. When we interviewed Yorlene in February, I asked the children to tell her about the work of a superintendent. She just added a few details.

Yorlene is a parent of two children and was pregnant with a third. We had already talked quite a lot at previous interviews about parenting, so Yorlene was able to take time to answer questions about her pregnancy. After that interview, we wrote a book about Yorlene. We used that book for two days during guided reading. Our only additional activity was to watch as Yorlene grew larger and larger.

In September, we interviewed Cameron's mother, Elisa, about her job in radio advertising. We wrote and read a book about Elisa. In June, while we were on a trip to interview workers on the Brooklyn Bridge, Elisa pulled out her cellular phone on the middle of the bridge so she could call Detroit to arrange an ad. The children understood that this was part of her job. Other than the homemade book and the related reading activities, there were no additional activities from this interview.

The same was true for the October interview of Alexander's mother, Jill. At the interview we role-played aspects of Jill's work as a travel agent. The information and concepts from the interview of Jill became the prior knowledge for the January interview of Farhan's father, Husain, who was also a travel agent. I asked the children to tell Husain what they knew about the work of travel agents. Then we were able to raise new issues and go into greater detail about Husain's job. We had a great discussion about the use of computers for getting information for customers about the weather conditions and flight information. Also, we had time to talk about child labor in Pakistan where Husain grew up. We wrote and read homemade books about Jill and Husain but had no further specific activities based on these interviews.

In December we interviewed Laura's mother, Leslie, who had been in the publishing business years ago. Leslie brought in some beautiful nature books she had worked on. Step by step, we role-played the process of publishing one of her nature books. After the interview we wrote a homemade book about Leslie. We kept the interview in mind as we continued to publish our own books at Writing Workshop. We brought that information with us when we visited Monique's godmother, Claudia, at Scholastic Books in January. In March, when we interviewed Susie's grandmother, an author, she was pleased to see how much the children knew about research and publishing. In May, we interviewed Eliza's mother, Susan, who works at a newspaper. She was happy to know that she didn't have to explain about such elementary things as dummies (the mock up for a page).

Whom Did We Interview?
Here is a list of the people we interviewed for People at Work from the first week of school in September until the last week in June.

Alexander's mother, Jill*—travel agent

step-grandfather, Walter*—retired, now an amateur artist

grandfather, Panka***—doctor, visiting from Florida

step-grandmother, Sandy***—retired teacher, visiting from Florida

Alina's mother, Yorlene*—building superintendent and pregnant
      mother

father, Ken*—building superintendent and maintenance worker for
      Amtrak

Allegra's grandmother, Constance**—maker of dollhouse furniture

Barbara***—staff developer, college teacher, visiting our school,
      grandmother was a sweatshop worker

Bobby*—sanitation worker, friend of classroom volunteer, Dora

Cameron's mother, Elisa*—in radio advertising

grandfather, Jack**—retired store manager, visiting from
      Connecticut

grandfather, Pooka**—shoe store owner

grandmother, Mary**—homemaker, visiting from Connecticut

Canaan's father, Michael*—director of a soup kitchen and homeless
      shelter. We conducted the interview at the homeless shelter.

family friend, Paula***—pediatrician working at the National
      Institute of Health, visiting from Washington, D.C. Paula deals
      with health and safety issues.

Courtney's mother, Denise*—customer service supervisor, Parking
      Violations Bureau

Daniella*—a first grader from Layne's class. Daniella spoke about her
      hearing impairment.

Daniel's father, Roger*—worker at a social service agency for senior
      citizens, also a frisbee champion

grandmother, Debby****—an educator and leader in the alternative
      school movement.

Eliza's mother, Susan*—editor at a major newspaper

father, Michael*—writer, teacher of journalism in a college

grandmother, Estelle**—retired teacher at a school for deaf children

Emily Arnold McCully****—author. We produced a play about her
      book, *The Bobbin Girl.*

---

* a full interview and a homemade book about the interview
*** grandparent participated in the Grandparent's Day interview at
Manhattan New School in November and is in our homemade book called* Our
Grandparents.
*** a full interview, but no homemade book about the interview
**** a quick interview, no notes, no homemade book

Farhan's father, Husain*—travel agent, also spoke about child labor in his country, Pakistan

Gloria*—aunt of Dora, grandmother of former student. Gloria makes artificial flowers for weddings and other events.

Ida*—security guard at Manhattan New School. Ida participated in the sit-in at Woolworth's in Greensboro, NC, 1960.

Jeffrey's mother, Gladys*—housekeeper at the Helmsley Palace Hotel

Jessica's father, Fred*—(2×) We interviewed Fred once about his job as an artistic director and another time about his mother's job in a sweatshop.

grandfather, Raymond***—Raymond talked about his former job producing Decca Records. Also, he talked about his father's work as a coal miner in Pennsylvania.

Johannah's mother, Beth*—psychologist

friend of Johannah's family, Diane*—teaches at the Lexington School for the Deaf

Jonathan's mother, Gloria*—orthodontist's assistant

Laura's mother, Leslie*—former publisher and teacher

father, Larry*—attorney

grandmother**—worker at the United Nations, also a neighborhood activist. She came also for a special interview about the local and successful struggle to keep a super Toys R Us out of the neighborhood.

grandfather, Jack**—retired oil worker

Lee's mother, Crescenciana*—former child laborer, currently a sweatshop worker in a garment shop. Lee was in my previous class.

Luca's mother, Colleen*—photographer

father, Elio*—restaurant owner

grandmother, Doreen*—former teacher for forty-five years, currently an actress, visiting from California

Melisa's mother, Esma*—building superintendent

Michael's father, Azi*—college teacher, teaches engineering

---

a full interview and a homemade book about the interview
**grandparent participated in the Grandparent's Day interview at* *Manhattan New School in November and is in our homemade book called* Our Grandparents.
***a full interview, but no homemade book about the interview*
****a quick interview, no notes, no homemade book*

Mr. Z****—Michael's mother's friend we interviewed at a construction site

Ken*—Michael's mother's friend, a builder of restaurants

Monique's godmother, Claudia***—editor at Scholastic Books. We interviewed Claudia and her colleagues at her job.

Nat's mother, Alison*—actress

father, Rusty*—musician

grandmother, Alice****—homemaker

Neil's mother, Susan*—international banker

Nicholas' mother, Monique*—administrator at the Metropolitan Museum of Art. We interviewed Monique at school and visited her at the Met.

father, Steve*—music producer at Sony Music Studios. We interviewed Steve at school and visited at work.

grandmother, Frances**—retired, formerly sold recycled rags and had a store with materials for sewing, visiting from Massachusetts

babysitter, Kathy*—talked about her mother's work as a quilter

Nico's father, Jorge*—a photographer and a Chibcha Indian whose family is from the rain forest of Columbia. Nico was in my class four years ago. Jorge's brother currently does photography of the rain forest region.

Nigel's mother, Pauline*—former child care worker, now on disability

Paula's mother, Anne***—retired special education teacher, currently an author, visiting from Buffalo, NY

father, Milton***—retired optometrist, currently a social documentary photographer, visiting from Buffalo, NY

Rafi's mother, Nancy*—writer and ghost writer. Wrote a book for Ben and Jerry.

Peggy and Doug*—farmer (Peggy) and manager of the distribution and sale of the farm products (Doug). They sell farm produce to Nancy and others in New York City.

Sheila's mother, Mary*—Irish folksinger and dancer. Mary works at the Irish Consulate. Sheila was in my class three years ago.

---

* a full interview and a homemade book about the interview
** grandparent participated in the Grandparent's Day interview at Manhattan New School in November and is in our homemade book called Our Grandparents.
*** a full interview, but no homemade book about the interview
**** a quick interview, no notes, no homemade book

Sophia's father, Eddie*—Union organizer for UNITE, the garment
workers' union. Sophia is from Julie's first-grade class at MNS.
Sophie's father, David*—musician, producer of jingles
mother, Abra***—actress. We interviewed her about conditions and
customs in the 1800s in Massachusetts, the setting for our play
about *The Bobbin Girl*.
Susie's father, Michael*—customer service worker for cable TV
grandmother, Lucille*—author of many books
Suzannah's mother, Jean*—co-founder and co-director of a
parenting center
father, Fred*—worker in customer service at the Department of
Transportation
John****—worker at the Brooklyn Bridge. The interview was
arranged by Suzannah's father.
Vickie*—paraprofessional in a special education class at MNS*

After the Interviews—Two Useful Teaching Tools

Homemade Books

After a full interview, we take a short break, then begin work on a
homemade book. Usually the writing is done right after the interview.
If there is no time, we write the book the next day. We talk briefly
about what we can write about the person. I encourage children to focus on one topic from the interview, although that is not a requirement. Children refer back to their notes to get ideas for their writing
or to remember details. It's another way for children to process information from the interview.

For the first book in September, most of the children draw pictures and dictate what they want to say to a student teacher or myself.
After the second or third book, most of the children write by themselves, using invented spelling. Sometimes the adult jots down in standard English on the back of the page what the child wrote so we can
interpret their invented spelling at a later time.

---

* a full interview and a homemade book about the interview
** grandparent participated in the Grandparent's Day interview at
Manhattan New School in November and is in our homemade book called Our
Grandparents.
*** a full interview, but no homemade book about the interview
**** a quick interview, no notes, no homemade book

All year we work on these strategies for spelling the words in the homemade books:

- Refer back to the interview journal.

- Refer to the words on the dry-mark board.

- Remember sight words and phonics from reading.

- Refer to the wall dictionary, which has sight words from this and prior interviews and reading activities.

- Use the classroom environment to copy words and names you need from signs, murals, labels, cubbies, and homework boxes.

- Sound out words.

As I walk around the classroom I stop to observe and to help. This is a good time to assess a child's comprehension and writing skills. If the child's writing does not relate to the interview, we talk about how to solve that problem. If a child has trouble spelling a

Melisa

Larry was telling us about his job. He is a lawyer. He helps people. He takes care of Laura and Steven. If someone has a problem they call Larry. They tell him what happened. Then Larry comes. Then they talk. When they're done talking, Larry has to go to the court. In the court they solve their problem
8 the end

Melisa's page from the homemade book *Laura's Dad, Larry* (June).

word, we sound it out together or look for that word somewhere in the classroom. In September or October we may just skip the word and move on to the next.

Any book we use for guided reading must be in standard English. At home I prepare the homemade books for publication, translating each page into standard English at the bottom or the top of the page. Later in the year, when the children's writing is more developed, I simply go over their words with a felt-tipped pen, making only a few corrections. At the beginning of the year there is a minimum of writing. By the end of the year the children pride themselves on writing pages "filled to the brim" with writing and no pictures at all. Then preparing the books for publication is more time-consuming. Family members or student teachers sometimes help.

Usually I cluster the pages with similar topics. Sometimes the children sort the pages of our books into categories before I number the pages. When the pages are clustered like this, vocabulary words are repeated over and over. Reading the first page of a cluster may be a challenge, but reading the second and third pages is easy. For instance, in the book about Alina's father, Ken, there were nine pages about his job at Penn Station, six pages about his job as a building superintendent, and seven pages about Ken as a father and a building superintendent.

As I prepare a homemade book for publication, I plan how to use that book for guided reading. Which strategies can best be developed— using the pictures, prediction, finding patterns, remembering words from previous pages, skipping words and then returning to them, or breaking difficult words into syllables? Would this book be especially useful for developing a particular phonics skill? Which new sight vocabulary is repeated most often? Is the book filled with compound words or contractions? Are there a large number of quotation marks? Then I must select only one or two for focus during guided reading.

We have been lucky in being able to have one copy of the books for each child made without charge at a friend's print shop. However, if we didn't have this opportunity, I would do everything possible to raise money to reproduce the homemade books.

Our homemade books are used at guided reading lessons two days a week. After use in school, children take the books home, read them to their families, practice specific strategies, work on skills, and discuss the details of the interview. An adult has to sign the cover indicating that the child has read the book to a family member. The signed books are returned to school on Fridays with the rest of the week's homework. I mark the cover to show that I have seen and appreciated their work at home. Some books come back with signatures from many friends and relatives, so that I know the child has read the book to many people. Finally, I send the book home again to be part of the family library.

Murals

Our classroom is filled with the spirit of our thematic study. There are murals everywhere. Mural making is a standard part of our curriculum. We make a new mural nearly every week. It's a way to connect art, social studies, and other curriculum areas. Murals help the children process information about an issue. They help build understanding. They help me evaluate whether children understand the information or issues.

Most of our murals are on ten-foot-long sheets of unwaxed white or brown butcher paper. The paper can be stapled or taped to a corkboard or cardboard from a huge box. We protect the floor by covering it with oilcloth and newspaper. The children wear painting smocks, which are old T-shirts from my three sons or from class families. Generally I recommend painting the background colors first so that drips and other problems can be painted over easily. We let the background dry and return to the mural the next day. At Center Time we gather near the mural to discuss the content, and then children draw the pictures with crayon. Next, we paint. I usually paint with the children. This gives us a further opportunity to discuss the content and issues depicted in the mural. Also, I can teach the children to use the materials well, and I can promote cooperation.

Our murals are done with paint, crayons, felt, Plasticine, construction paper collage, or a combination of these materials. For a collage mural, after painting the background, we color pictures on white paper, then cut and glue them to the mural. This is particularly useful when we want to show details. When we made a Jackie Robinson mural, we painted a baseball diamond in the background. Then we made baseball players from Plasticine and glued them onto the mural.

We made a felt-on-felt mural. This was a lot of work. Vicky's mother, Milagros, directed the project, and other parents helped out over several weeks. We made an overall plan. Then research groups worked with adults to plan the details of their panels.

Usually the children make signs describing the content of the mural. Because I want the children to practice reading with standard English, I write a standard English translation at the bottoms of the signs.

Our mural about the removal of garbage to the landfill.

We always put completed murals up in the classroom. We refer to them frequently. Sometimes we add details as our research continues. After a while, some murals are hung in the hallways.

The Interdisciplinary Nature of the Curriculum

After an interview I look to see which skills can be taught and for the essence of what the person said. What were the key issues or values raised at the interview? How can this person become more deeply involved with our class? How can we keep the concepts alive in an interdisciplinary curriculum?

Doing the Planning

The activities in the weeks and months after an interview help build a greater depth of understanding of the content of the interview and are designed to develop skills. I like to show student teachers different ways of doing this kind of planning and curriculum development. Sometimes we construct a chart listing age-appropriate activities for extending the content into various curriculum areas. During and after the interview, I think about how we can do this. I talk with colleagues, student teachers, and family members. Critical to determining how to proceed are the particular interests of the children and their families.

We must take into account their ongoing questions and interests as well as the other factors discussed in previous chapters. Following are examples from our People at Work study.

A Homeless Shelter

Canaan's father, Michael, worked seven days a week at Holy Trinity Church, where he directed a homeless shelter on the weekends, a soup kitchen, a senior lunch program, and an afterschool center. We interviewed Michael at his job so that we could see some of the programs in operation. Michael took out his guitar and sang with us. We presented flowers we had made to the senior citizens. I made notes for planning experiences beyond Michael's interview.

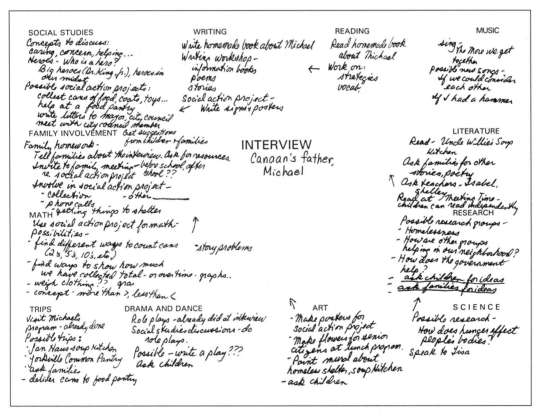

Paula's planning notes from the interview with Michael, Canaan's father.

Following are the concepts I developed and the interdisciplinary activities we did related to the interview of Canaan's father.

Key social studies concepts in the interview.   Michael's is a life of caring about and helping others. People who help others are heroes in our community. You don't have to be world famous to be a hero.

Writing.   Each child wrote and illustrated a page for the homemade book about Michael. We talked about heroes when we were naming our book. We thought about "What is a hero?" We talked about major heroes in history such as Martin Luther King, Jr., and Rosa Parks. Then we talked about heroes in our community such as Michael. We thought about heroes in our school. The children thought of the principal, Shelley, and the other teachers who had started our school. They thought of the security guard, Ida, who was in the civil rights movement. We decided to call the book *Michael Is Our Hero*.

Reading.   We used our book *Michael Is Our Hero* for two days. We worked on this strategy for figuring out difficult words:

- Skip the word.

- Continue reading to the end of the sentence.

- Look at the word and think about what word would make sense.

- Make a guess.

- Check your guess by looking at the spelling of the word.

- Reread the sentence and decide whether the word makes sense.

Literature.   At Meeting Time I read *Uncle Willie and the Soup Kitchen* (1991), a picture book by Dyanne DiSalvo-Ryan. It's a story about a young boy who goes with his uncle to a soup kitchen where the uncle volunteers. Whenever possible I look for a story related to the topic of the interview. I also look for poetry or nonfiction.

Family involvement.   In *Family Homework* the week before, I had invited families to join us on the trip to Holy Trinity Church. Several parents joined us. For homework, children read *Michael Is Our Hero* to their families and discussed the interview. I told the families about the reading strategy. I invited the families to come to an early morning meeting to think about how our class could help homeless people. Three parents came to the meeting, and we had a great discussion.

Social action.   My class thought of ways they could help people who are homeless. Then we looked at the ideas from the family meeting and came up with a plan. For two months we would collect winter coats and cans of food for programs for the homeless in the area. We invited the whole school to participate. Families got involved in many ways.

Math.   Our social action project quickly evolved into a math experience. Each day we counted the cans. When we started getting lots of cans, counting by ones took too long, so we rearranged the cans and counted them by twos, by fives, and by tens. Each day after counting, we recorded the number of cans on a chart. We had well over one hundred cans by the end. A group of students worked with a student teacher to sort the clothing. Some people had given us items besides the coats, so we sorted by types of garments.

Art.   For several days at Center Time a group of children painted a mural about Michael's homeless shelter. I was able to assess how much the children had learned from the trip and the interview by listening to the discussions during the planning and painting stages.

Disabilities
Pauline, Nigel's mother, had taught at a child care center until she became disabled. Now she gets government disability assistance. We role-played and discussed the jobs Pauline did at the child care center. Pauline told us that she wanted to work but was unable to do so because of back problems. We discussed how the government sometimes provides money for people who are disabled.

Key social studies concepts in the interview.   Some people are disabled. This means something different for each disabled person. Here a few issues that could flow from the interview:

- The person can no longer do the work she used to do.

- The person may have to learn a different kind of job.

- Some bosses do not want to hire people with disabilities.

- Some people cannot work at all.

- The government sometimes helps people who are not able to earn enough money to live.

- There are organizations or groups that help disabled people.

- People have worked together to get laws to protect the right of the disabled to work.

Over the course of the school year we would get involved with each of these issues, some in a superficial way, others in a substantive way.

Research.   Two groups of children began to do research about disabilities during Reading and Research Workshop. One group worked with a student teacher and did extensive research about people who are blind and about seeing-eye dogs. A few months later, I worked with another group, which did research about people who are hearing-impaired. This led to an interview of Diane, a teacher of hearing-impaired children at Lexington School for the Deaf. Diane talked about her job, about the job placement program at her school, and about the difficulties of finding work when you are hearing-impaired. She lent us two videos for people who are hearing-impaired, a TTY telephone, and a book about hearing-impaired children. We practiced sign language.

We interviewed Daniella, a first grader from another class, who is hearing-impaired. When a parent volunteer had tested all the children in our school, she had found that Daniella had a hearing problem in one ear. Now Daniella wears a hearing aid. She discussed her disability with us.

Dora's brother and niece are deaf. We talked informally with Dora about this. As a child, Dora went to some classes at a school for the deaf so that she could learn how to communicate with her brother. We observed Dora, Diane, and Johannah's mother communicate in sign language.

Several children had relatives with hearing aids. In *Family Homework* I encouraged children to interview those relatives. They interviewed them by telephone, some even long distance. They had never thought about discussing the hearing aids because they thought it might upset the person. Susie came to school with notes from an interview with her grandmother, who is hearing-impaired. It turned out that the relatives really enjoyed speaking to the children about their hearing impairments.

Writing and art. The children wrote and illustrated pages for the homemade book about Pauline.

Reading. When the book, *Pauline, Nigel's Mother*, was published and each child had a copy, we used it for guided reading for two days. Because there were many words ending with *ing*, we used this book to focus on *ing* words. We also worked on the strategy of looking at pictures to help us figure out difficult words. This also gave us the opportunity to discuss issues from the interview again.

Science. Lisa, the science teacher, had been teaching about the parts of the human body. During the interview with Pauline, I drew a picture of the spine. Then Pauline showed the children how her spine was curved, making it so difficult for her to stand for long periods of time. Very often, when science topics came up during interviews, Lisa and I thought together about how we could extend these topics beyond the interview.

Family involvement. Families were told about the interview with Pauline in *Family Homework* and were asked to discuss the issue of disabilities with their child. Some families ended up talking about disabled people in their extended families for the first time. I asked families to help us contact other people with disabilities who might come for an interview.

The children took the book *Pauline, Nigel's Mother* home to read to families. They did a homework worksheet about *ing* words. The worksheet had poetry filled with *ing* words. I wrote about and encouraged the families to help their child use the strategy of looking at pictures to help figure out difficult words.

Working Conditions

Alison talked about her work as an actress. She acts in plays, does voice-overs in ads, and reads books on tape. Alison spoke using some of the voices from shows in which she acted. She told us how she learned to speak in those voices. We enjoyed hearing her speak with the Yorkshire accent of the "maid" she played in *The Secret Garden*. Later in the year she would call Nicholas' mother, Monique, to learn to speak in a German accent for another show. Monique is from the Netherlands and speaks several languages, including German. We would learn more about that from Luca's grandmother, Doreen, an actress from California. The children already knew a lot about parenting, so Alison just talked briefly about that.

Nat's mother, the actress Alison Fraser (left), with Paula at an interview.

Key social studies concepts in the interview.   Alison explained that actors and actresses usually do several different kinds of jobs in order to make a living. It's not always easy. At subsequent interviews, we found that other family members from our class worked at two or three jobs in order to make ends meet. This was quite a shock to some children and a way of life for others.

After the interview I asked Alison if she would help us produce a play about *The Bobbin Girl,* by Emily Arnold McCully. This is a book I had been reading with a research group during Reading and Research Workshop. Sophie's mother had sent this book to school, thinking it might be useful in our People at Work study. The book takes place in a cotton mill in Lowell, Massachusetts, in 1834. It's about the bad working conditions at the cotton mills, the use of child labor, and the struggle to improve working conditions. Alison went home that day and began to write the play *Let's Stick Together.* There were quite a few social issues that flowed from our experience with the play:

- Child labor.

- Sweatshop working conditions.

- Work-related illnesses.

- Long ago, some people tried to improve their working conditions.

- Some people have worked to get new laws to protect people from dangerous or unhealthy working conditions, to end child labor, and to get higher pay.

- People are still trying to end sweatshop conditions and child labor. We can join them.

Drama, music, and social studies. During the interview Alison told us about auditions. Then we role-played an audition. When Alison and I were selecting children for parts in *Let's Stick Together,* we had our own informal audition. Alison practiced our play with us more than twenty-two times. Often she rushed to or from our class to auditions, rehearsals, or performances. Nat's father, Rusty, who is a musician, helped with the music and directed rehearsals when Alison was not available. The children performed the play at our first family celebration that year. The families honored Alison for her tremendous effort.

At both of our family celebrations Sophie's father, David, sang folksongs about the mill workers.

Nicholas' father, Steve, actually recorded *Let's Stick Together* during our trip to Sony Music Studios, where he works. Steve and his colleagues produced a video of the play, weaving into it photographs from Russell Freedman's book, *Kids at Work: Lewis Hine and the Crusade Against Child Labor* (1994) and pictures from *The Bobbin Girl.* Children and adults sang along as we watched the video at the family celebration in the spring. Steve made a copy of the video for each family. The play became a unifying factor in class and among the families.

Research and literature. Early in the year I contacted the author of *The Bobbin Girl,* Emily Arnold McCully, through her publisher. In the late spring, she came for a brief visit to the class. With only one day's notice, the children presented *Let's Stick Together* to her as well as our mural about sweatshops. The children interviewed her and asked numerous very sophisticated questions about how and why she does so much research for her books about history. Afterward the families arranged a reception. She signed autographs and promised to return to the school next year for a longer visit.

Research. A rather large research group formed. For nearly one month it met during Reading and Research Workshop to learn more about child labor and sweatshops. Children wrote down their questions in their reading and research journals. They wanted to know if the children could go to school, how old the child laborers were, and what kinds of health and safety problems the children faced. We thought about where to get more information. The group started by rereading *The Bobbin Girl* with me and looking at Lewis Hine photographs. I showed the young researchers how to use the index of *Kids at Work* to find the pages that would answer their questions. Then I held the book so they could watch as I read the text. The children were pleased to find many words they already knew. We discussed and role-played the content. We read articles families had clipped from newspapers and magazines. They shared this information each day with the whole class. I shared it with the families in *Family Homework.*

Sophie's mother, Abra, spoke to the whole class about living and working conditions in the mills of the 1800s. We looked at clothes from the period. This helped us prepare costumes for our play.

Crescenciana, the mother of a former student, came for an interview. She had been a child laborer in Mexico and now works in a sweatshop in New York City. She talked about working conditions. She told about when the workers, with the help of their union, walked out of the shop for two days the previous year because the boss made them wash the bathrooms and refused to install proper lighting. We role-played that walkout. Crescenciana came to class to volunteer during a period of lay-off from the factory.

When we told a visitor, Barbara, about our interest in sweatshops, she told us that her grandmother had worked in a sweatshop. We brought her over for a quick interview.

The families knew about our study from reading *Family Homework* and talking with their children. Suzannah's father, Fred, told me about Eddie, the father of a first grader from another class. At his interview, Eddie spoke about the work of his union, UNITE, which is trying to eliminate sweatshop conditions and child labor in the United States.

Eddie told us about the Triangle Shirtwaist fire. Then Amy, a graduate student who was helping in the class, brought us a book about that fire, *Fire at the Triangle Factory* (1996), by Holly Littlefield. The book was about the terrible working conditions at a garment factory that led to the fire. It was also about bigotry among the families of the factory workers, people of different nationalities and religions. Despite the prejudice of their families, some of the young girls working at the factory developed friendships and saved each other's lives. For many months the class had done research and activities about these different issues, so reading this book was a very powerful experience for all of us. The children voted unanimously to give up much of their Center Time so that we could finish the book that day. In the next *Family Homework* I told the families about this book. Some of the families already knew about the fire and discussed it at home.

A friend from UNITE had sent us a special edition of *Weekly Reader* about child labor. There was a picture of young children stitching soccer balls in Pakistan. One article provided addresses and

Canaan's page from the homemade book *Eddie Works for a Union*
(May).

encouraged children to write letters. The American Federation of Teachers had a special article encouraging teachers to involve our classes in the campaign to end child labor in the production of soccer balls. When Farhan's father, Husain, came for his interview, the children asked him about this. Husain told us more about the use of child labor in Pakistan.

Math. Both our play and the interview with Crescenciana dealt with the concept of time. In our play, the boarding house owner rang the bell at 4:30 a.m. so the workers could get up for work at the mill.

Crescenciana talked about her schedule when she was a child in Mexico:

5:00 a.m.—get up and make tortillas
5:50 a.m.—walk many miles to school
12 noon—walk home from school, then cook lunch
1:00 p.m.—begin work in the fields until evening

These were perfect opportunities to practice telling time and discuss a social issue. At Math Workshop we did that and practiced using a.m. and p.m.

Social action. I wanted the children to understand that their play was a form of social action. It influenced the many people who saw it. In addition, several children wrote to Nike and to the manufacturers of soccer balls to complain about their use of child labor. They received a reply. During the year, the federal government set up meetings with representatives of labor unions and employers to develop standards about child labor and working conditions. The children saw that our class was part of a growing worldwide effort and that they were partly responsible for the new guidelines.

Writing and art. Each child wrote and illustrated a page for the book *Alison Is an Actress: A Story About Nat's Mother.* At Writing Workshop children wrote many stories about sweatshops and child labor during the year. A group of children painted a mural about sweatshops.

Reading. For two days at Reading Time, we used the homemade book about Alison. Children searched the book for *ing* words. We worked on the strategy of prediction. I asked, "What would you expect to find in a book about Alison?" Children suggested we would find the words *actress, act, sing,* and *show.* I wrote those words on the dry-mark board, and the children wrote them in their reading and research journals. Because the children have been at the interviews, they know the content of the homemade books. When one has an idea about what one might find in a book, the reading becomes much easier. We would use this strategy before reading all the rest of our homemade books and trade books. This book had many words with the *ing* ending. We practiced adding *ing* to words.

Health and science. *The Bobbin Girl* and our play, *Let's Stick Together,* made us aware of brown lung disease, a dangerous illness caused by the damp, lint-filled air in the cotton mills. We became interested in this medical issue.

At about the same time we did research about the cotton mills, a group of children was doing research about the work of coal miners. They worked on this, day after day, for nearly two months during Reading and Research Workshop, using as resources photographs, books, magazines, and people.

It turned out that four members of our class were from coal-mining families. I would never have known this about my students if I hadn't communicated regularly with the families through *Family Homework.* Nicholas' mother, Monique, stopped by to tell about her relatives from the Netherlands who had been miners. Jessica's grandfather, Raymond, came for an interview to tell us about his father who had been a coal miner in Pennsylvania. Canaan's father came by to sing coal-mining songs during Meeting Time. Andrew's mother, Cheryl, told us about her family of coal miners in West Virginia. Each told us about black lung disease, which affects coal miners. The children quickly hypothesized that the brown lung and black lung diseases were similar because they were both caused by dust in the air.

At Center Time the researchers built their own coal mine in the block area. Plastic train tracks wound their way into the block coal mines, where there were lumps of real coal. Some of our miners took time to attach wires from batteries to switches to tiny light bulbs. They attached these lights to construction workers hats before they entered their mine.

We talked and role-played stories about people working to get new laws to make the mines safer for the workers. Eddie talked about this at his interview. Also, a friend of Canaan's family came to our class for an afternoon interview. She was visiting New York City but worked in Washington, D.C., for the National Institute of Health. She discussed the health issues from our play with us. She told us about how products and medicines are tested for safety. We role-played how people work to get new laws to protect people from unsafe products and medicines.

Family involvement. In *Family Homework* I told the families about the interview with Alison and kept them fully informed as we continued our research about child labor and sweatshops. I asked for resources for the research. Several parents came with us to the Sony Music Studios. Families helped their children read and practice their scripts. Over 125 family members, babysitters, and friends came to each of the two family celebrations. Each family contributed to the feasts. When we had a breakfast the last day of school, I asked the adults to sing the songs from our play without the children. They knew all the words.

All of these activities flowed from the interview with Alison. The role playing and adult-assisted research were crucial. But the most significant factor was the interviews, where real people presented information directly to the children.

Ravages of War

Esma, Melisa's mother, is a single parent with three children. Her husband died in the United States when the children were babies. At the interview we heard that Esma worked very hard as a parent and as the superintendent of three buildings near our school. Esma came from Yugoslavia to find a better life. She hated war because she saw how war has ruined her country. At the interview we role-played the Dayton Peace Accord, which was signed the year before.

Key social studies concepts in the interview. Being a single parent is a big job. War hurts and kills people. There are more peaceful ways to resolve problems.

Music. When Esma told us about Yugoslavia, we role-played the Dayton Peace Accord. It reminded the children of Ed McCurdy's song "Last Night I Had the Strangest Dream." In the song the people come together to sign a treaty saying they will never fight again. We sang it for her.

Literature and Writing. At Meeting Time we read Shel Silverstein's poem about peace, "Hug O'War," from *Where the Sidewalk Ends.*

Each child wrote and illustrated a page for our book about Esma. We worked on focusing the writing on one topic and providing details. Some children wrote only about Esma's country. Others wrote only about Esma's job as a superintendent. Some wrote about Esma as a parent. When I prepared the book for publication, I clustered these topics.

Reading. We used the book about Esma, *Melisa's Mother*, for guided reading for two days. One of the reading skills we worked on was using commas. We noticed that when there was a list of animals Esma had when she lived in Yugoslavia, there was a comma after each animal. Jonathan wrote, "Esma's family had a farm. They had horses, cows, dogs, pigs, and cats." We stopped for a moment when we got to the commas. Later in the book, Johannah wrote, "A super has to fix things. Here is a list: pipes, toilets, sinks, and bathtubs."

Also we used the strategy of predicting what would be on the pages about the farm, or what would be on the pages about Esma's being a superintendent. Those predictions were based on the children's memories of the interview.

Family involvement. In *Family Homework* I told the families about the highlights of our interview with Esma. They hadn't known much about her and how hard she works. I told the families about our discussion of the Dayton Peace Accord and of the song "Last Night I Had the Strangest Dream," which some of the parents already knew.

For homework the children read our book about Esma to their families. Also, they did a worksheet about commas. The worksheet had sentences from the homemade book as well as poems with lots of commas.

Social action. Some of the children were so moved by the interview that they decided to write to President Clinton urging him to work for peace. They received letters and stickers saying "I wrote to the President, and he wrote back."

A Newspaper

Susan, Eliza's mother, is a deputy editor at a major newspaper. At the interview she talked about how people must work together to prepare a newspaper. She showed us a dummy for the front page of her newspaper and explained how people from the various departments meet daily to discuss and debate which articles will go on the front page. I wanted the children to see that process. During the interview, we pretended to write articles, and we role-played the front-page meeting.

Key social studies concepts in the interview. It was important for the children to interview a woman who held a high position at her place of employment. Many times during the year, the children had discussed the issue of people being excluded from jobs because of race or gender. Children read a number of easy-to-read picture books about this topic.

People must work together to produce a newspaper. It is not always easy. We could apply the example of the front-page meeting to many other work situations.

Writing and art. Instead of writing a book about Susan, we made our own newspaper, *407 Times.* The children wrote and illustrated articles for the different sections: sports, national news, metropolitan news, science, health, and so on. We gathered at story circle for an editorial meeting to determine the contents of the front page. We made a dummy. We included a special series of articles about sweatshops that had been written as part of a *Family Homework* assignment.

Reading. *407 Times* was our guided reading lesson for two days. We developed further the strategy of using prediction. We found that we could look at each section of the newspaper and predict what words we might see. For example, in the sports section, we predicted that we would find words such as *baseball, hockey, ice skating,* and *Mets' Stadium.* We wrote these words in our journals. Sure enough, there were such topics. There was even an article about our family trip to the Jackie Robinson Memorial Game at Shea Stadium. We would use this same strategy after looking at the title of each chapter in a chapter book.

Family involvement. In *Family Homework* I told families about the interview with Susan and asked them to discuss it at home. For homework children had to read *407 Times* with their families. They had to teach their families about using the prediction strategy when reading different sections of our newspaper.

Assessment

How do I know whether the children understand what was said at an interview? What tools do I have to assess their learning? Samples of the

407 Times

Volume I ....Number 1 copyright 1997, 407 Times   NEW YORK, TUESDAY, MAY 20, 1997   50 CENTS

*Sign from sweatshop protest,
New York City, photo by Michael
Heskiaoff*

Sweatshops, As Seen By First Graders

by Alina Vukelj

NYC, May 16 - In some kinds of sweatshops there can sometimes be a fire. Workers get very little pay. Sometimes the windows are nailed shut. The workers hardly get a break. Sometimes, it's very damp . There is so much lint in the air. The workers can hardly

continued on p. 4

Researchers To Present Their Play About George Washington Carver

City Desk

NYC, May 16 - Only in first grade, and they are already doing research. Can you imagine that? Their play about George Washington Carver will be presented for the first time on May 20 at the MNS Theatre. The play tells of Carver when he was a child. Slave robbers

continued on page 6

Class Parent Runs Homeless Shelter

by Canaan Folk Reinke

NYC, May 16 - In the homeless shelter at Holy Trinity Church they let homeless people sleep. But during the day, the homeless people have to go. When it's dark, they can come back. The shelter is open on Fri-

*Typical Weekend at homeless shelter.
Drawing by Canaan Folk Reinke.*

continued on page 2

New York Times Deputy Foreign Editor Inspires Class to Write This Newspaper

by Michael Heskiaoff

NYC, May 16 - Students in room 407 interviewed Eliza's mother, Susan Chira, before she rushed off to work at the *New York Times*. Susan told us about her job. She is in charge of the news from other countries. We decided to write our own newspaper, *407 Times*. We had to debate about what would be on the first page.

MNS Class Joins Jackie Robinson Celebration At Shea Stadium

City Desk

Queens, May 16 - In April, more than 50 children and their families from room 407 went to Shea Stadium to attend the Jackie Robinson Memorial Game. Principal Shelley Harwayne was interviewed at MNS by Channel 5 reporters just before boarding the bus. She thought it was so important to honor Jackie Robinson because he helped break the color bar in baseball. He was the first African-American person to play in the Major Leagues. A group of researchers presented a play, *A Man With A Dream*, right on the sidewalk for the reporters! The play was written by the first grade researchers with help from the student teacher from New York University, Jonathan Landau. The

*Jackie Robinson at his first Major
League baseball game.Drawing of
Jackie Robinson by Laura Profeta*

continued on page 7

The front page of *407 Times*, May 20, 1997.

children's work become part of the portfolio. I discuss the portfolio and my observations at two formal family-teacher conferences, at numerous informal conferences in the classroom, on the telephone, or in the schoolyard. Working closely with families regarding assessment is essential.

Assessment at the Interview

Is a child asking any questions? What kinds of questions does a child ask? Is a child able to follow a line of questioning at an interview? For example, when Bobby is telling us the details about his job as a sanitation worker, are the questions focused on those details? After I shift the focus to a discussion about Bobby's role as a parent, are children able to shift their questions? How skilled are children in thinking of and formulating questions? Has a child started to ask more substantive questions over time? Are children able to generalize or to find commonalities? I listen carefully.

At the interview, I watch to see where and how children choose to sit. Are they focusing on the interview or the role play? Are they participating? Are they taking notes when I ask them to, or do they wait for a personal reminder? I discuss these matters with their families.

Assessment During Small- and Large-Group Discussions

My favorite assessment tool is to see how children use information from an interview to help them understand other topics and issues. Do they see connections to literature, music, art, or other events in history?

During the discussions, I want to see the depth of understanding. I look for analytical skills. There is always a growing number of children who indicate their depth of understanding by making connections. I listen for this during small-group and whole-class discussions and when a child discusses something with me. I want to see whether children are able to use information from one interview at future interviews.

When it's time for a small-group discussion, do the children actively turn to the one or two children next to them and engage in a conversation? Or do they wait for me to bring them into a group? I watch to see how well children communicate with each other. Do they listen to each other? Do they make eye contact? Are they talking with or at each other?

Assessment During an Art Activity

Before the children work on their pages for the homemade book, we always talk about the possibilities for topics for the pages. Yet there will be children whose drawings indicate a partial or complete lack of understanding of the information. Others may make illustrations so filled with details or so relevant that they indicate a great depth of understanding.

Looking at the content of the murals, at small paintings and drawings, and at the art work on the pages for the homemade book helps me assess children's understanding. I listen to the conversation during the planning stages of the mural. Usually I paint alongside the children, so that I can participate in that conversation and assess children's understanding.

During the People at Work study, a group of children did research about artists. They wrote down a list of questions. Day after day during Reading and Research Workshop we looked through art books. We asked family members who were in the room during the workshop to tell us what they knew about the particular artists we were studying. I wrote about our research in *Family Homework* and asked for resources. Children brought more books and pictures from home.

When the children said that Vincent Van Gogh was "crazy" because he cut off his ear, we had an excellent discussion about mental illness. We talked about how Van Gogh did suffer from mental illness but that at that time there were no medicines to help him. This discussion helped me assess this area of understanding. We took time to examine Van Gogh's use of colors in his paintings. When we looked at one of the paintings, the children wrote down in their reading and research journals all the colors in the water, the sky, and the grass. During the next two weeks at Center Time the researchers chose to paint two Van Gogh–like murals—one of the irises and the other of the starry night. When I painted with the children, it was clear to me how much each child understood Van Gogh's use of color and was able to make a first-grade replica.

The researchers saw how Jacob Lawrence told the story of the Great Migration. They liked to show Jacob Lawrence pictures to anyone they could so they could explain the story. At Center Time they painted a mural of people waiting at the train station for the trains going to the big cities in the North. The mural talk helped me assess their understanding.

When the researchers looked at a book about Picasso, they noticed the different periods of his work. They were fascinated by the cubist period. Suzannah's mother, Jean, had stopped by for a brief visit. I asked her to help read and look through one of our Picasso books with the children. One day, during Reading and Research Workshop we took time to make a huge "Junior Picasso Cubists" mural. Each of us chose a spot on a large sheet of butcher paper and colored pictures in the cubist style. The "mural talk" was great. Some children showed a good range of abilities while coloring in this style.

Assessment During a Writing Activity

The content of the writing for the homemade book provides a clear indication of the depth of understanding, even the writing done in invented spelling. Some children stay focused on the actual interview while other children actually make up or have erroneous information.

I look at the actual writing skills. Are children using pictures, or have they moved on to words, phrases, or sentences? How effectively are they using the classroom environment to help them with spelling?

Some children choose to write about the interviews during Writing Workshop. Again, their written compositions can be used to evaluate their understanding. In fact, some of these books will become part of a child's portfolio.

Assessment Through Reading and Literature

I observe children at reading time. Do they apply their prior knowledge to the reading experience? Are they developing strategies for becoming independent readers?

I listen for comments during a literature discussion, "That reminds me of . . . [a story or poem]." I know that making these connections indicates understanding. Also, it indicates that children are retaining and using information. When Nat's father, Rusty, played his accordion during his interview, it reminded one of the children of the accordion in *Something Special for Me*, by Vera B. Williams.

Laura's grandmother, Marion, told us at her interview about the community effort to stop a megastore from being built in our school neighborhood. A child commented that it reminded her of Judith in *The Bobbin Girl*, because Marion and Judith both tried to make things better for people.

Assessment Through Music

Quite often a child will say at an interview, "That reminds me of . . . [a song]." By the end of the school year, these references to songs are very common and tell me a lot about the children. Any mention of the word *coal* brought a response, "Can we sing 'Sixteen Tons'?" Any mention of markets brought a chorus of "Can we sing 'Linstead Market'?" If the word *tally* came up during a math activity, someone would want us to sing "Day-O," in which the tally man counts the bunches of bananas the workers have picked.

Often we write our own songs or adaptations of songs we know. I watch as children suggest lines for the songs. Are the words relevant? Do the words fit the pattern of the song?

For some children, music is a central part of their being. If that is true for a child, is the family aware of it, and do they nurture that love of music at home? How can I encourage that?

Assessment at Reading and Research Workshop

In this inquiry-based classroom there is constant research during Reading and Research Workshop. Comments or discussions at interviews can spark an interest in a topic. Children can pursue those interests by doing research. I watch to see how children use the available books, atlases, maps, and other research tools in the classroom. Do they bring materials from home? Are they able to use the materials and then record information in their journals? Can they do this independently? How do they function in a research group with or without adult supervision? Are they able to share the information with the class? Are they able to do projects to share their information—murals, small or big books, shoe box movies, dioramas, posters, or block building?

Assessment at the Dressup Corner or Block-Building Area

During our People at Work study, there was a several-week research project about slavery. We had just interviewed Vickie, whose college dormitory had been the home of abolitionists. I saw a bunch of children crawling under a table and hiding there. Some children rushed over to me to ask if I had seen any runaway slaves. I said I hadn't. The quality of the retelling during dramatic play is another way to assess understanding.

After the construction site interviews I noticed children bringing toy hammers and other tools to class. They made their own construction site in the block area. You could tell that they had been listening and observing very carefully.

Assessment for the Future

We enjoy the world of learning that has evolved from our classroom interviews. As an educator, my greatest concern is whether the children will apply these critical thinking skills in the future. Will the children continue to ask questions and seek answers? Will they continue to inquire, whether or not it is encouraged at home or at school? Will they continue to see themselves as researchers? Will they continue to cherish their youthful thoughts about justice and peace? Will they act on their knowledge? So many questions, so many particulars.

Bibliography and Resources

Professional Reading

Allen, JoBeth, Barbara Michalove, and Betty Shockley. 1993. *Engaging Children: Community and Chaos in the Life of Young Literacy Learners.* Portsmouth, N.H.: Heinemann.

Banks, James. 1975. *Teaching Strategies for Ethnic Studies.* Boston: Allyn and Bacon.

———. 1996. *Multicultural Education, Transformative Knowledge, and Action.* New York: Teachers College Press.

———. 1997. *Multicultural Education: Issues and Perspectives.* Boston: Allyn and Bacon.

Bigelow, Bill, and Linda Christensen. 1994. *Rethinking Our Classrooms: Teaching for Equity and Justice.* Milwaukee: Rethinking Schools.

Bigelow, Bill, and Norm Diamond. 1988. *The Power in Our Hands: A Curriculum on the History of Work and Workers in the United States.* New York: Monthly Review.

Burns, Marilyn. 1992. *Math and Literature (K–3).* White Plains, N.Y.: Math Solutions Publications.

Covington Smith, B. 1989. *Women Win the Vote.* Englewood Cliffs, N.J.: Silver Burdett Press.

Curriculum Frameworks: Knowledge, Skills, and Abilities. Grades Pre-K–12. 1995. New York: New York City Board of Education.

Derman-Sparks, Louise. 1989. *Anti-bias Curriculum: Tools for Empowering Young Children.* Washington, D.C.: National Association for the Education of Young Children.

Doherty, Jonathan L. 1981. *Women at Work: 155 Photographs by Lewis W. Hine.* New York: Dover Publications.

Freedman, Russell. 1994. *Kids at Work: Lewis Hine and the Crusade Against Child Labor.* New York: Scholastic.

Gomez, Aurelia. 1992. *Crafts of Many Cultures.* New York: Scholastic.

Graves, Donald H. 1985. *Writing: Teachers and Children at Work.* Portsmouth, N.H.: Heinemann.

Hamston, Julie, and Kath Murdoch. 1996. *Integrating Socially: Planning Integrated Units of Work for Social Education.* Portsmouth, N.H.. Heinemann.

Harwayne, Shelley. 1992. *Lasting Impressions.* Portsmouth, N.H.: Heinemann.

Hunter, William A., ed. 1974. *Multicultural Education Through Competency-Based Teacher Education.* Washington, D.C.: American Association for Colleges of Teacher Education.

Kivel, Paul, and Allen Creighton. 1997. *Making the Peace: A Violence Prevention Curriculum.* Alameda, Calif.: Hunter House.

Kobrin, David. 1996. *Beyond the Textbook: Teaching History Using Documents and Primary Sources.* Portsmouth, N.H.: Heinemann.

Kostelnick, Marjorie J., ed. 1991. *Teaching Young Children Using Themes.* Glenview, Ill.: HarperCollins.

Kozol, Jonathan. 1992. *Savage Inequalities: Children in America's Schools.* New York: HarperCollins.

Kruse, Ginny Moore, and Kathleen Horning. 1991. *The Multicolored Mirror: Cultural Substance in Literature for Children and Young Adults.* Madison: University of Wisconsin. Available from Highsmith, P.O. Box 800, Fort Atkinson, WI 53538-0800.

Lewis, Barbara. 1991. *The Kids Guide to Social Action.* Minneapolis: Free Spirit Publishing.

Loewen, James. 1995. *Lies My Teacher Told Me: Everything Your American History Textbook Got Wrong.* New York: Simon and Schuster.

Logan, Judy. 1993. *Teaching Stories.* Plymouth, Minn.: Minnesota Inclusiveness Program.

Multicultural Guide: An Annotated Bibliography. 1995/96. New York: New York City Board of Education. This guide has extensive listings for all grades.

Nieto, Sonia. 1996. *Affirming Diversity: The Sociopolitical Context of*

Multicultural Education. White Plains, N.Y.: Longman Publishing Group.

Perry, Theresa, and James Fraser, eds. 1993. *Freedom's Plow: Teaching in the Multicultural Classroom*. New York: Routledge.

Pigdon, Keith, and Marilyn Woolley, eds. 1993. *The Big Picture: Integrating Children's Learning*. Portsmouth, N.H.: Heinemann.

Preece, Alison, and Diane Cowden. 1993. *Young Writers in the Making: Sharing the Process with Parents*. Portsmouth, N.H.: Heinemann.

Rich, Dorothy. 1987. *Teachers and Parents: An Adult-to-Adult Approach. School and Families: Issues and Actions*. Washington, D.C.: National Education Association.

Rochman, Hazel. 1993. *Against Borders, Promoting Books for a Multicultural World*. Chicago: American Library Association Books/Booklist Publications. This book has an extensive annotated listing for middle and high school.

Rogovin, Milton. 1995. *Triptychs: The Lower West Side of Buffalo, Revisited*. New York: W.W. Norton. Social documentary photographs and oral history.

Rogovin, Milton, and Michael Frisch. 1993. *Portraits in Steel*. Ithaca: Cornell University Press. Social documentary photographs and oral history.

Schniedewind, Nancy, and Ellen Davidson. 1983. *Open Minds to Equality: A Sourcebook of Learning Activities to Promote Race, Sex, Class, and Age Equity*. New York: Prentice Hall.

———. 1987. *Cooperative Learning, Cooperative Lives: A Sourcebook of Learning Activities for Building a Peaceful World*. Dubuque, Iowa: William C. Brown Co.

Schulke, Flip, ed. 1976. *Martin Luther King, Jr., A Documentary . . . Montgomery to Memphis*. New York: W.W. Norton.

Short, Kathy, and Jerome Harste. 1995. *Creating Classrooms for Authors and Inquirers*. Portsmouth, N.H.: Heinemann.

Sunshine, Catherine, and Deborah Menhart, eds. 1991. *Caribbean Connections: Puerto Rico*. Washington, D.C.: Network of Educators' Committees on the Americas.

Takaki, Ronald. 1993. *A Different Mirror: A History of Multicultural America*. New York: Little, Brown.

Tchudi, Stephen, and Stephen Lafer. 1996. *The Interdisciplinary Teacher's Handbook*. Portsmouth, N.H.: Heinemann.

Turner, Tillie. 1989. *Take a Walk in Their Shoes.* New York: Dutton.

UNICEF. 1997. *The State of the World's Children.* New York: Oxford University Press.

Wilks, Susan. 1995. *Critical and Creative Thinking: Strategies for Classroom Inquiry.* Portsmouth, N.H.: Heinemann.

Zaslavsky, Claudia. 1993. *Multicultural Mathematics: Interdisciplinary Cooperative-Learning Activities.* Portland, Maine: J. Weston Walch. This is for grades 6–9.

———. 1994. *Multicultural Math: Hands-on Math Activities from Around the World.* New York: Scholastic.

———. 1996. *The Multicultural Math Classroom.* Portsmouth, N.H. Heinemann.

Zinn, Howard. 1995. *A People's History of the United States.* New York: HarperCollins.

Prose for Children

Barber, Barbara E. 1994. *Saturday at the New You.* New York: Lee and Low Books.

Coles, Robert. 1995. *Story of Ruby Bridges.* New York: Scholastic.

Cowen-Fletcher, Jane. 1994. *It Takes a Village.* New York: Scholastic.

De Paola, Tomie. 1981. *Now One Foot, Now the Other.* New York: Putnam's Sons. Also see other books by Tomie de Paola.

DiSalvo-Ryan, Dyanne. 1991. *Uncle Willie and the Soup Kitchen.* New York: William Morrow.

Fitzpatrick, Marie Louise. 1991. *The Sleeping Giant.* Cooleen Dingle, County Kerry, Ireland: Brandon Books.

Golenbock, Peter. 1990. *Teammates.* New York: Harcourt Brace Jovanovich.

Hoban, Tana. 1997. *Construction Zone.* New York: Greenwillow Press. Also see other books by Tana Hoban.

Hoffman, Mary. 1991. *Amazing Grace.* New York: Dial Books.

Jakobsen, Kathy. 1993. *My New York.* New York: Little, Brown.

Jaspersohn, William. 1996. *Timber! From Trees to Wood Products.* New York: Little, Brown. Also see William Jaspersohn's books about other workers: baseball player, marine biologist, TV news reporter, veterinarian, magazine publisher, motorcycle manufacturer, airline pilot.

King, Laurie, ed. 1994. *Hear My Voice: A Multicultural Anthology of Literature from the United States.* Reading, Mass.: Addison-Wesley. For secondary school readers.

Kunhardt, Edith. 1996. *I'm Going to Be a Vet.* New York: Scholastic.

Lindbergh, Reeve. 1996. *Nobody Owns the Sky: The Story of "Brave Bessie" Coleman.* Cambridge, Mass.: Candlewick Press.

Lionni, Leo. 1973. *Swimmy.* New York: Knopf. Also see other books by Leo Lionni.

Littlefield, Holly. 1996. *Fire at the Triangle Factory.* Minneapolis: Carolrhoda Books.

McCully, Emily Arnold. 1996. *The Bobbin Girl.* New York: Penguin. Also see other historical fiction by Emily Arnold McCully.

Meltzer, Milton. 1988. *Starting from Home.* New York: Puffin Books. Also see Milton Meltzer's historical fiction and nonfiction books.

Mohr, Nicholasa, and Antonio Martorell. 1995. *The Song of El Coqui and Other Tales from Puerto Rico.* New York: Penguin.

Oz, Charles. *How Does Soda Get into the Bottle?* New York: Simon and Schuster.

Pomerantz, Charlotte. 1989. *The Chalk Doll.* New York: HarperCollins. Also see other books by Charlotte Pomerantz.

Rankin, Laura. 1991. *The Handmade Alphabet.* New York: Scholastic.

Steptoe, John. 1987. *Mufaro's Beautiful Daughters: An African Tale.* New York: Lothrop, Lee and Shepard. Also see other books by John Steptoe.

San Souci, Robert D. 1989. *The Talking Eggs.* New York: Dial Books.

Williams, Sherley A. 1992. *Working Cotton.* New York: Harcourt Brace.

Williams, Vera B. 1984. *Music Music for Everyone.* New York: Greenwillow Books. Also see other books by Vera B. Williams.

Yin, Chamroeun. 1996. *In My Heart, I Am a Dancer.* Washington, D.C.: Network of Educators' Committees on the Americas.

Poetry, Music, and Food

Agard, John, and Grace Nichols, eds. 1994. *A Caribbean Dozen: Poems from Caribbean Poets.* Cambridge, Mass.: Candlewick Press.

Bell, Janet. 1991. *The Black Family Reunion Cookbook: Recipes and Food Memories.* New York: Simon and Schuster.

Blood, Peter, and Aurelia Patterson. 1992. *Rise up Singing: The Group Singing Songbook.* Bethleham, Pa.: Sing Out Corporation.

Brecht, Bertolt. 1947. *Selected Poems*, ed. H.R. Hays. New York: Grove Press.

Burgie, Irving. 1992. *Caribbean Carnival: Songs of the West Indies.* New York: William Morrow.

Cullinan, Bernice, ed. 1996. *A Jar of Tiny Stars: Poems by NCTE Award-Winning Poets.* Honesdale, Pa.: Wordsong, Boyds Mills Press and National Council of Teachers of English.

DeFina, Alan A. 1997. *When a City Leans Against the Sky.* Honesdale, Pa.: Wordsong, Boyds Mills Press.

Delacre, Lulu, comp. 1989. *Arroz Con Leche: Popular Songs and Rhymes from Latin America.* New York: Scholastic. This book includes songs, games, and rhymes that will be familiar to families from Latin America. The songs are in Spanish and English.

———. 1990. *Las Navidades: Popular Christmas Songs from Latin America.* New York: Scholastic.

Driving Hawk Sneve, V., ed. 1991. *Dancing Teepees: Poems of American Indian Youth.* New York: Scholastic.

Greenfield, Eloise. 1986. *Honey, I Love and other love poems.* New York: HarperCollins.

———. 1988. *Nathaniel Talking.* New York: Black Butterfly Children's Books.

Greer, Colin, and Herbert Kohl, eds. 1995. *A Call to Character: A Family Treasury of Stories, Poems, Plays, Proverbs, and Fables to Guide the Development of Values for You and Your Children.* New York: HarperCollins.

Gunning, Monica. 1993. *Not a Copper Penny in Me House: Poems from the Caribbean.* Paintings by Frané Lessac. Honesdale, Pa.: Wordsong, Boyds Mills Press.

Hudson, Wade, and Cheryl Hudson. 1995. *How Sweet the Sound, African-American Songs for Children.* New York: Scholastic.

Hughes, Langston. 1994. *The Dream Keeper and Other Poems.* New York: Scholastic.

Joseph, Lynn. 1990. *Coconut Kind of Day.* New York: Puffin Books.

Lessac, Frané, ed. 1978. *Caribbean Canvas.* New York: Lippincott. Also see other books by Frané Lessac.

The Lion and the Lamb, Peace Arts Center, Bluffton College, 280 West College Avenue, Bluffton, OH 45817-1196. Curriculum ideas and resources about social issues.

Meyers, Walter Dean. 1993. *Brown Angels.* New York: HarperCollins.

Miller, E. Ethelbert, ed. 1994. *In Search of Color Everywhere: A Collection of African-American Poetry.* New York: Stewart, Tabori and Chang.

Silverstein, Shel. 1974. *Where the Sidewalk Ends*. New York: Harper
and Row.

———. 1981. *A Light in the Attic*. New York: Harper and Row.

Singer, Marilyn. 1989. *Turtle in July*. New York: Macmillan.

Slier, Deborah. 1996. *Make a Joyful Sound: Poems for Children by
African-American Poets*. New York: Scholastic.

Solomon, Jay. 1991. *A Taste of the Tropics, Traditional and
Innovative Cooking from the Pacific and Caribbean*. Freedom,
Calif.: Crossing Press.

Wenner, H., and E. Freilicher. 1991. *Here's to the Women: 100 Songs
for and About American Women*. Portsmouth, N.H.:
Heinemann.

Resources

Children's Creative Response to Conflict, Box 271, Nyack, NY
10960. This group works not to abolish conflict but to enable
children to deal with it creatively. Teacher resources, a
newsletter, and courses.

City Lore: The New York Center for Urban Folk Culture, 72 East
First Street, New York, NY 10003. Tel.: (212) 529-1955.

Educators for Social Responsibility. 23 Garden Street, Cambridge,
MA 02138. Tel.: (617) 492-1764. Discussion of issues,
curriculum ideas, and resources.

Highsmith, P.O. Box 800, Fort Atkinson, WI 53538-0800. Tel.:
(800) 558-2110. Extensive catalog of multicultural books.

Maryknoll Educational Resources, Maryknoll, NY 10545-9989.
Tel.: (914) 762-0316. Extensive resources for teaching about
Africa, Asia, Latin America, Central America, and the
Philippines.

National Association for the Education of Young Children, 1834
Connecticut Avenue N.W., Washington, DC 20009-5786. Tel:
(800) 424-2460. Educational programs, a newsletter, and
extensive resources for early childhood.

National Association for Multicultural Education, 1511 K Street,
N.W. #430, Washington, DC 20005.

National Coalition of Educational Activists, P.O. Box 679,
Rhinebeck, NY 12572. Tel.: (914) 876-4580. *Rethinking
Schools* newsletter has information about school reform and
resources. This organization is composed of parents and
educators involved in school reform.

Network of Educators' Committees on the Americas, P.O. Box

73038, Washington, DC 20056-3038. Tel.: (202) 238-2379.
Antiracist and multicultural resources for K–12. Among
NECA's very useful resource guides in the *Caribbean
Connections* Series are *Overview: Puerto Rico, Jamaica, and
Haiti, Teaching About Haiti; Overview of Regional History:
Jamaica, Puerto Rico.*

Resource Center of the Americas, 317 17th Avenue, Minneapolis
MN 55414-2077. *Connection to the Americas* (newsletter),
multicultural and bilingual resources for educators and youth,
and curriculum ideas.

UNICEF, United Nations, 3 UN Plaza, New York, NY 10017.
Curriculum materials and resources.

United States Committee for UNICEF, 333 East 38 Street, New
York, NY 10016. Tel.: (212) 686-5522.

Acknowledgments

I want to thank the many people who have guided me in becoming a parent, a friend, an activist, and an educator:

My parents, Anne and Milton Rogovin, who gave me love and moral support, a social conscience, and inspiration for my teaching.

Ellen Rogovin Hart, teacher, wonderful sister, and friend, who has always been there for me, and to her daughters Malaika and Aliza. My brother, Mark Rogovin, a dream-keeper.

My sons, David, Steven, and Eric, who since babyhood pre-viewed the books I read to my classes, heard my school talk each day at the supper table, marched with me in demonstrations, and brought joy to my life. Thank you for your patience while I have written this book, while I have planned for my teaching, and while I have partici-pated in the day-to-day stuff of social action.

The members at the Teachers College Writing Project, who have changed the direction of my teaching.

Shelley Harwayne, who believed in me and taught me to think of a teacher as a researcher, and who insisted that it was time for me to join the staff at Manhattan New School. Thank you, Shelley, for insist-ing that I take notes each day so that I could write this book. Thank you for creating Manhattan New School, which for me has meant working in an environment where I can give true meaning to the con-cept of inquiry-based multicultural education.

My colleagues at P.S. 132 and P.S. 173, where I taught for twenty years, who gave me friendship and support, and the paraprofessionals with whom I shared the work and the joys—Iris, Judith, Doris, and Marlene.

My co-workers, past and present, at Manhattan New School: the teachers—Regina, Lisa, Isabel, Lorraine, Layne, Joanne, Pam, Carmen, Diane, Sharon, Judy, Kevin, Dawn, Joan, Debby, Eve, Cindy, Denise, Renay, Pamela, Michael, Julie, Roberta, Constance; the custodial staff—John, Gonzalo, James, Alfredo, Neil; the paraprofessionals—Vickie, Pat, and Maria; the cooks—Azzalee and Pat; the security guard—Ida; the secretary—Judy; the administrative assistant—Tara; the school aides—Pauline and Beatrice. A special thanks to my colleague Regina for your friendship and help with this book.

The families of my students, who have been my co-workers and friends; Nilda, Waleska, Magaly, Sheila, Jane, Joan, Mary, Theresa, Alison, Fred, and so many other parent/grandparent volunteers; and the Parent-Teacher Associations that live and breathe for their children.

Dora Cruz, grandmother of Kathy, volunteer, co-worker, and friend. You have enriched my life and the lives of many children.

My friends, Becky Berman, Linda Brown, Janice and Ed Dabney, Gail Gordon, Eileen and Liam O'Toole, Eileen and Jim Gilbert, Marla Mikelait, Maria Munive, Francia Rivera, Angela Napoli, Ann Sadowsky, Seth Segall, Hallie Wannamaker and Vincent Brevetti, and Karol Kilimnik.

My best friend from high school, Mary Segall, still best friend, educator, and author—thank you.

My friend Minetha Spence, a hospital worker with whom I rode the bus to work for ten years and the car pool for the last four years. You have taught me what I know about your country, Jamaica, the songs and the stories. Your friendship and kindness are an inspiration.

Georgia Heard, who helped me love to teach children to write poetry. The many poets who write for children—Eloise Greenfield, Langston Hughes, Monica Gunning, Lynn Joseph, Marilyn Singer, Walter Dean Meyers, and others. You have brought happiness into my classroom.

Jay Friedman, my son Eric's first-grade teacher in Teaneck. Thank you for the several years our classes were pen pals. This gave me an opportunity to work with an educator who is deeply involved in multicultural education. Thanks for helping me with this book.

Lori Wolf, who observed in my classroom a few days each week as you prepared your doctoral thesis. Thanks for hearing me think out loud about multicultural education.

Lois Bridges, my editor and now friend at Heinemann.

Those student teachers who opened their hearts and minds to the children and to inquiry-based learning. I am happy to have worked with you and I hope you will spread the message.

The many education activitists who are leading the struggle for school reform and progressive education.

My heroes Harriet Tubman, Martin Luther King, Jr., Fannie Lou Hamer, and Nelson Mandela, and the millions of lesser-known heroes in schools and communities around the world.

The nearly seven hundred students in my classes over the past twenty-four years. I love you and thank you for the joy you have brought to my life.